Group Power II:

A Manager's Guide to Conducting Regular Meetings

William R. Daniels

Pfeiffer
& COMPANY

Amsterdam • Johannesburg • Oxford
San Diego • Sydney • Toronto

This book is printed on acid-free, recycled stock that meets or exceeds
the minimum GPO and EPA specifications for recycled paper.

PREFACE

The weekly staff meeting is a problem for many managers. It seems necessary, yet it never seems to have much vitality. Members often show signs of reluctance to attend, boredom during the process, and an eagerness to leave. If such meetings are important, why do they feel this way? What is wrong?

As a matter of fact, these regular meetings are important. The ability to lead them has been recognized as one of the critical skills of effective management. We know that for some managers these meetings really do promote clarity of purpose and teamwork. But why they work for some managers and do not for most has not been widely understood.

The usual recommendation has been to get the members involved in problem solving. Research about group work reveals that this is usually exciting work for groups, and that success in problem solving will lead to mutual respect and team morale. But recent observations of effective managers find that they are not doing problem solving in their regular meetings. As Rensis Likert suggested nearly thirty years ago, they usually delegate this activity to task forces.

What effective managers are doing in regular meetings is exercising the organization's formal power. The members are required to share in the leader's review of operations and authorization of change. In most cases, the analysis of the issues and the recommendations for action have been carefully formed by staff experts and task forces prior to the meeting. And usually the members have been well educated about the issues prior to the meeting. So why is the meeting necessary? Why isn't it just a useless "going through the motions"? Because the regular meeting is where ideas are transformed into organizational reality; it is the regular meeting that invests them with power.

The regular meeting is a unique and necessary event. It is the next step beyond problem solving—something that the task force or expert staff cannot accomplish. It is the step by which the organization's intelligence gets integrated into its operations—the step where the service of staff is transferred to the active authority of line. It is "only a ceremony," but until such ceremonies take place, the organization cannot act responsibly.

When managers become conscious of the distinction between task forces and regular meetings—between the cognitive and ceremonial functions of meetings—they can restore both groups to their rightful functions. The principles and procedures for managing the two kinds of meetings are as different as their purposes. Management effectiveness depends upon knowing how to run both types of meetings.

This book, based on two years of field research, summarizes the principles and procedures for leading regular meetings. (My first book, *Group Power: A Manager's Guide to Using Meetings*, summarizes the principles and procedures for running task forces.) This book, like the other, is divided into three sections:

The Basics—a summary of the principles behind leading effective regular meetings.

Procedures—specific, step-by-step ways to lead the group through its work.

Activities—activities that will help a manager train his or her group members for effective participation in regular meetings.

Our field work has already involved testing of these recommendations (and more testing is under way). It has been exciting to see how consistently regular meetings have been revitalized through the use of these principles and procedures. The revitalization is not mere novelty or hype. The members pay attention because they understand the vital importance of what they are doing—that they are handling the organization's power and its ability to commit itself to action.

The regular meeting becomes an event! It is no longer a mere distribution of information or a bored "overhearing" of the boss's one-on-ones with peers. It becomes the time and place where the human resources of the organization are reoriented, focused, empowered. It recaptures all the affirming and transforming force that ceremony has always provided for the human community. The regular meeting becomes the secular organization's ceremony of power.

William R. Daniels
Sausalito, California

August 1989

ACKNOWLEDGMENTS

Many people have been involved during the last several years in making this book possible. Especially important in the beginning has been the financial and administrative support of the San Diego Regional Training Center. Bud Emerson, Executive Director, and the Board of Directors (composed of City Managers within San Diego County) typify the generally progressive leadership being exerted in public administration in their part of the world. They provided two essential ingredients:

- A variety of organizations within which to make our observations;
- Highly qualified volunteers who devoted significant time to being trained and to making field observations.

Of the more than ten cities that made themselves available for our studies, special thanks is offered to Ron Bradley, City Manager, and his entire management team at the City of La Mesa where some of our most "intrusive" observations have been made; their patience and cooperation were crucial.

During the first two phases of the project sponsored by the Center, the following volunteers were especially helpful in designing and implementing the work:

Phase I

John Fitch	Frank Mannen	Bill Workman
Steve Wheeler	Bob Toone	Jeanette Farris
Rod Wood	Ann Moore	Jim Thompson
Robin Reid	Trudy Sopp	

Phase II

Jody Richard	Ruth Ann Hageman	Nancy Acevedo
E. MacGregor-Jones	Lucy Bubb	Christine Morrison

For more than double duty during Phase II, special thanks to:

Anne Rast	Shirley Mills	Corinne Wong-Miller

It was possible to interest several private enterprise clients in the project. Their review of the findings and their additional observations broadened the data base and increased our confidence in the recommendations. Special thanks to Neal Jensen at Baxter

Healthcare Corporation, to Sue Thompson and her staff at Levi Strauss & Company, to Patrick Wilson and Linda Thompson at Amdahl Corporation, and to Christine Oster and Capri Langford at Intel Corporation.

I am grateful for the encouragement received in discussions of the data during the 1986 Annual Consortium sponsored by the Saltwater Institute in Santa Cruz, and at the "Meeting of Exalted Chosen Ones," sponsored by the National Society for Performance and Instruction at their 1986 National Convention.

Many people have read and commented on the manuscript and it now reflects their influence. Special thanks must be offered to Lynn Kearny, Michael Kelly, and Tom Justice, all of whom returned the manuscript with so many questions and marginal comments that serious rewriting was provoked.

Finally, I have to thank my colleagues who secured the contacts for this work through American Consulting & Training, Inc.: Lila Sparks-Daniels, Frank Potter, Judy Viccellio, and Linda Silvestrini —and again to Linda and to Nan Maples in their roles as AC&T consultants for ongoing encouragement and refinement of the work.

Lila, my wife the President, deserves special credit for getting the manuscript in shape, for sensitive encouragement, and for keeping the work in context so that life was enjoyed during the process.

While I bear responsibility for the way in which our discoveries are described in this book, I hope all of those who have been involved will sense some pride of authorship.

CONTENTS

Preface   iii
Acknowledgments   v

Part 1: The Basics   1
  The Functions of Regular Meetings   3
    Two Kinds of Meetings: A Preview   3
    The Exercise of Formal Power   4
    The Theater of Corporate Culture   9

  Leading the Regular Meeting   10
    Controlling the Agenda   11
    Structuring the Permanent Membership   15
    Maintaining Appropriate Dynamics   18
    Guiding the Process   24
    Providing a Memory System   31

  Participating in Regular Meetings   32
    Attitudes   32
    Participant Skills   33
    Critical-Thinking Skills   34

Part 2: Procedures   37
  Agenda Building   39
  Bin List   43
  Expected Response   45
  Case Studies   47
  Performance-Plan Review   49
  Operations Review   53
  Leader's Plan Update   57
  Recommendations Review   61
  Start/Stop/Alert   65
  Highlights/Lowlights   67
  FYI Posters   69
  For the Good of the Order   71
  Problem Definition   73
  Assignment Matrix   77
  Flea Market   79
  +/− Meeting Evaluation   83

Part 3: Activities   85
     1: Screening the Agenda for Regular Meetings   87
     2: Structuring Membership of Regular Meetings   95
     3: Recognition Methods   101
     4: Identifying Participant Skills   105
     5: Participant Skills Assessment   109
     6: Operations Review Meeting 1   113
     7: Operations Review Meeting 2   121
     8: Start Up Staff Meeting 1   131
     9: Start Up Staff Meeting 2   139
    10: Task-Force Review   147
    11: Recommendations Review   151

Appendix   155
     Ceremony and Power   157
     Answers to Activities   163

Bibliography   171

Part 1:
The Basics

THE FUNCTIONS OF REGULAR MEETINGS

Two Kinds of Meetings: A Preview

There are two kinds of meetings that a manager needs to be able to lead: **Task Forces** and **Regular Meetings**[1]

Task forces are formed to do the initial, in-depth study of complex problems, decisions, and plans. Only the few necessary experts are members. The dynamics and processes are rational discussion among peers. The outcome is group intelligence.

Regular meetings are called for the purpose of exercising the organization's formal power. These meetings evaluate the organization's operations, identify needs for change, authorize attention to these needs (often through task forces), approve recommendations for action, and allocate the resources that make the organization's mission a reality.

To call a meeting "regular" not only connotes that it is held on some fixed schedule, it means that the meeting exercises the power of "regulation." Regular meetings control the organization's performance. Within organizations, regular meetings are typically called "departmental/management meetings," "staff meetings," "project review meetings," "standing committees," and "commission/council meetings."

Regular meetings always display, affirm, and exercise the organization's values, structures, and roles—so they are also the primary means by which the organization perpetuates its culture.

---

[1]The distinction between task forces and regular meetings is not commonly recognized. However, Rensis Likert in his classic work, *The Human Organization: Its Management and Value*, 1967, New York: McGraw-Hill, spoke of regular meetings as "work groups" (p. 50) and task forces as "ad hoc" committees or work groups (p. 70). The only serious attention to this distinction in current literature as far as the author knows is *High Output Management* (pp. 71-87) by Andrew S. Grove, 1985, New York: Random House. Grove calls regular meetings "process-oriented" meetings, and task forces "mission-oriented" meetings (p. 72).

A large amount of research has been done on the dynamics and processes of small groups. Most of the findings have their greatest usefulness in the leadership of task forces. A summary of these findings for managers was presented in my earlier book, *Group Power: A Manager's Guide to Using Meetings.*

It is unfortunate that so little research has been done on regular meetings. As it turns out, they absorb the most time and create the greatest amount of frustration and unhappiness, especially the weekly staff meeting. The subject clearly needs attention, and that is the purpose of this book.

In 1985, with the assistance of the San Diego Regional Training Center, directed by Bud Emerson, an effort to understand the dynamics and processes of regular meetings was begun. After two years of field observations and field testing, our research project confirmed at least two things:

1. *Regular meetings are very important.* They are essential to managing an organization's performance and culture. Properly led, these meetings clarify the purposes and ground rules for human interaction (a powerful psychological need for everyone). Well led, regular meetings assure responsible control of organizational power, a key to human survival.

2. *Regular meetings are unique.* The attempt to lead regular meetings based on the findings of most of the earlier research about small groups is a mistake. Their dynamics and processes are not the same as those of a good problem-solving group. Furthermore, it appears unlikely that the same people will be able to perform the purposes of task forces and regular meetings at the same time; it is helpful to separate the two meetings.

The distinctions between task force and regular meetings are listed in summary fashion in Figure 1. This summary serves as a preview of the suggestions made in this book. These suggestions are made in the spirit of continuing exploration. Try them; see how they work for you. If they do not work, try to understand why, and then try something else.

The Exercise of Formal Power

The primary function of regular meetings is to exercise organizational power.

	Task Force	**Regular**
Function	Superior intelligence.	Authorization; affirmation of organizational values, structures, roles.
Agenda	Problem analysis; decision analysis; planning.	Pass downs; operations review; recommendations review; news.
Structure	Only necessary experts; five to nine members only.	Appropriate functionaries; no numerical limits.
Dynamics	Equity; uninhibited access to every intelligence. (Use *inclusion* activity.)	Role differentiation; status affirmation. (Use *recognition* activity.)
Process	1. Build common data base; 2. Interpretation; 3. Resolution.	1. Presentation; 2. Review; 3. Decision; 4. Commissioning.
Memory	Flip charting; publishing.	Official records; symbols.

Figure 1. Two Kinds of Meetings

Organization and power always exist together. They depend on each other. The organization's resources are never sufficient to support all its possible goals, so a system must be created to control how the resources will be used. Such a system must have the power to withhold or take away resources from some parts of the organization and give them to others.

In order to prosper, the organization's control of its resources —its power—must be guided by complete and accurate information. The power must be focused on well chosen and clearly understood goals. There must be a way to monitor how well the organization is meeting its goals so that its power can be used to fix what does not work and take full advantage of its successes. And the organization has to have a way to learn about new opportunities and methods so that its power can be used to start new efforts. Without good information, the organization cannot use its power wisely.

How information is collected, distributed, interpreted, and employed for the organization's acts of power is at the heart of the management function. Management structure, procedures, and roles are all methods for getting information and power together. There is a variety of ways to get intelligence and power working together. But as organizations get larger and more complex, and as their external environments become more demanding, it appears that the best management systems involve effective regular meetings.

Effective regular meetings are held where information is delivered ready for action. They are the scenes where information is employed in acts of power. In the best management systems, it is in regular meetings that the organization's goals are determined, its operations judged, and its changes authorized.[2] In effective management systems, regular meetings are instruments for using the organization's power.

When regular meetings are deprived of authority, they become limp and lifeless—perceived by members as a more or less polite exchange of irrelevancies. After a few such meetings, the members usually show signs of boredom and irritation. Such meetings damage respect for the leader, the subjects discussed, the participants, and the whole organization.

Powerless regular meetings are most typically found in organizations where management is practiced in the classic one-on-one style. Under this style all decisions are made by the leader in private discussions with one subordinate at a time. When all the subordinates are brought together, they are essentially strangers to one another's work with nothing of significance to do as a group.

In one-on-one management systems, the agenda of the regular meetings usually consists of the leader's inquiries, announcements, and assignments. Each meeting is, in fact, a series of one-on-one meetings between the leader and one of the members. Having everyone in the same room for such a series of meetings may serve the leader's convenience, but it is often seen by the participants as

---

[2]See the presentation of "System 4" in chapter 4 of *New Patterns of Management* by R. Likert (1961), New York: McGraw-Hill. The superiority of System 4 and its use of meetings is again demonstrated in *The Human Organization* (see footnote 1), pp. 55-59. The Institute of Social Research at the University of Michigan has continued to substantiate both the superior effectiveness of System 4 and the importance of meeting leadership within it.

an irritating waste of time waiting for a turn. Such meetings can be enlivened a little with the procedures suggested in Part 2 for dealing with news, and they can be speeded up by using the procedure called "Flea Market." But until the leader sees the potential of group participation within his or her authority and invests the group with real power, the regular meetings will continue to exhibit the uninformed and uncooperative behavior inherent in one-on-one management.

Powerless regular meetings also occur where participants misunderstand their role as *representative.* In this management system, subordinates attend the leader's meeting solely to represent departmental concerns—to promote and protect the interests of their departments. Their opinions, when expressed, always serve this limited purpose.

If the leader invests authority in a representative group, the departmental interests of the members usually lead them to form coalitions and politically to subvert rational decision making. Unchecked, this factionalism eventually leads to the focus of resources in the most dominant coalition—which may not be what is required for the organization's common good. To guard against this possibility, or simply to avoid being politically outmaneuvered, the leader often holds on to the power. Because the advice of subordinates is too blatantly biased to be trustworthy or useful, the leader is usually driven to exercise authority in an autocratic fashion. Once again the regular meeting becomes a solo performance of the leader with occasional accompaniment by one or two other members.

The first step toward improving regular meetings is to *confront the issue of the meeting's authority.* What action is it empowered to take? What actions within the organization are under its control? The answer to both questions can be stated as follows:

The authority of a regular meeting is the same as that of its formal leader.

It is crucial for the leader to make this connection. To empower the meeting, the leader brings the members into the exercise of his or her own authority.[3] The leader does not give up power or in any way make it ambiguous. The members are made resources not only for implementing the leader's decisions (as in one-on-one

---

[3]*The Human Organization* (see footnote 1), p. 181.

management), but also as advisors and consultants who can inform the decisions. Getting group intelligence for the exercise of the leader's power is the whole point of effective regular meetings.

The second step toward improving regular meetings is to *require the members to participate in the leader's authority.* The members cannot be valuable advisors as long as they function only from within the limited concerns of their individual departments. They must be required to move into the larger domain of the leader's authority and responsibility for all the functions represented in the meeting. To require participation in the leader's authority is to require *participative management.*

Unfortunately, participative management has been represented as permissive—something managers allow subordinates to do. But participative management does not happen that way. It must be clearly stated as an expectation. Then it must be required! In the group and probably in private coaching sessions, the leader will have to make clear to the members that representative behavior is out, and that performance as a consultant to the leader is a criteria for each individual's formal evaluation.

One reason participative management must be required is that it has to have the sanction of the leader's higher authority. *Peers* cannot technically take responsibility for one another or submit to the evaluation and direction of one another. A manager is out of line when he or she attempts to direct a peer. Such an act violates the organization's intended distribution of authority. Peers can only reap the benefits of the group's exercise of authority (participative management) through the license of their superior. A manager is well within line when trying to influence a peer through the authority of their common superior, and especially so if such efforts are required by that superior.

Another reason participative management has to be required is that it places significant new demands on those in management. Participative managers are not only responsible for their own departments, they are also required to gain competence in all the areas of responsibility represented in the roles of their immediate superiors. Only as this wider competence is developed can they fulfill their responsibilities as participants in their leaders' authority.

In participative management, the engineer must learn the ways of finance; the chief of police must learn the ways of the public works director. These requirements explain why participative organizations are the most effective in leadership development and why they so characteristically promote from within—after all, they have no need to bring in an unknown to do a job for which they already have three or four experienced candidates—but these requirements also make participative management the most demanding of organizational cultures.

As the leader empowers the regular meeting, the meetings themselves become more vital and even exciting. More important, the entire organization represented in that regular meeting will be strengthened. Its power will be better defined, more accessible, more intelligently and swiftly employed, and exercised participatively.

The Theater of Corporate Culture

Because regular meetings are the organization's centers of power, they take on other functions. They provide a sort of stage on which the life of the organization and its leadership displays itself. Each meeting is a reminder of the fact that its members are bound together in a special way for a special purpose—that they have defined roles to play within a scheme of interrelated authorities and responsibilities. Regular meetings are a kind of theater that dramatically affirms the organization's entire culture:

Its mission;

Its values;

Its structure;

Its distribution of authority;

Its roles for human performance.[4]

Whether or not the leader is paying attention to this culture-reinforcing function of the regular meeting, the function will be performed.[5] A carelessly organized meeting that does not result in

---

[4]This point is taken from *Organizational Culture and Leadership: A Dynamic View* (p. 239) by Edgar Schein, 1986, San Francisco: Jossey-Bass.

[5]In "How an Organization's Rites Reveal Its Culture," Janice M. Beyer and Harrison M. Trice say, "Many practical managerial activities also act as cultural rites that are interpreted by employees and others as reflecting what management believes in, values, and finds acceptable. Unless consequences are considered, both the activities chosen and the ways of carrying them out may inadvertently convey cultural messages that are inconsistent with the desired culture." See J. P. Kotter (Ed.), *Organizational Dynamics* (p. 8), 1978, Reading, MA: Addison-Wesley.

action shows everyone a careless and impotent culture. The regular meeting that is only a solo performance of its leader shows a culture dominated by and dependent upon that individual. When the behavior of the regular meeting is a combative struggle to secure departmental advantages, a culture of intimidation and political self-serving is displayed. But where the regular meetings are an orderly review of the organization's performance—where the members are all thinking on behalf of the meeting's leader and the exercise of that person's authority—we see displayed a culture of participative management.

No mission statement or published organizational chart or public-relations effort is ever sufficient to overcome the message conveyed in the behavior of management at regular meetings. At regular meetings we see the organization's culture in action—its values transformed into the flesh, blood, and materials of reality. Everything else is just "good ideas," because behavior speaks louder than words; and the regular meeting is the behavioral statement of the organization's culture.

Never in history have human beings been able to improve the quality of their lives without organization, and never have we been able to maintain organizations without regular affirmation of their existence, authorities, and processes. In earlier times, this affirmation was achieved through religious ceremony. The hierarchy—holy order—was believed to be a sacred reality; the leaders within it were thought to be divinely ordained to exercise heavenly authority.

Over time, we have developed a different respect for organizations—we recognize both their power and their potential for enormous harm. They are not necessarily inspired nor are their leaders in any way superhuman. It is a configuration of roles bound together by thousands of tiny agreements within which massive resources are focused on the accomplishment of certain limited goals.

Regular meetings are the secular ceremonies by which these thousands of agreements are confirmed, by which the resources are ever more sharply focused, and by which the goals themselves are held up for scrutiny and commitment. *Regular meetings are a secular society's ceremonies of power.*

LEADING THE REGULAR MEETING

The leader of regular meetings has special responsibility in five areas:

1. Controlling the agenda
2. Structuring the permanent membership
3. Maintaining appropriate dynamics
4. Guiding the process
5. Providing memory systems

Attention to these five areas will allow the regular meeting to perform its function as an instrument of the organization's power and as a purveyor of the organization's culture.

It is often a good idea for the leader to use one of the members as a facilitator or to bring in a specialist in facilitation. The facilitator can assist the leader in planning the meeting and can devote complete attention during the meeting to maintaining the appropriate dynamics and using appropriate procedures. This should free the leader to focus more on the issues before the group. This can be especially helpful in large, complex meetings. (Using a trained facilitator is also a good way for leaders and members to develop their meeting skills.)

When a facilitator is used, the leader and facilitator must be clear about their roles and should make sure the group understands their roles. The facilitator assists the leader in running the meeting, and the best facilitators do most of this behind the scenes. It is especially important that the work of the facilitator support and amplify the authority of the leader. There should never be any question about whose meeting it is or whose authority is being exercised in the decisions of the meeting. From start to finish, in all five of the areas, the regular meeting is the responsibility of its leader.

Controlling the Agenda

Identify Appropriate Kinds of Agenda

It is important to give the participants at regular meetings the right kind of work to do. The regular meeting is not the right place for complex cognitive chores such as problem solving or planning; this should be done by task forces. Nor is it right to spend large amounts of time in educational or social activity. To exercise organizational authority, regular meetings only need to process four kinds of agenda:

- *Pass Downs:*[6] These are decisions or announcements that the leader brings to the meeting from other, higher centers of authority. The members are expected to understand the item and commit to implementing it. Through this activity, the regular meeting promotes compliance and coordination within the organization.

- *Operational Status Reports.* Each member of the meeting reports the status of the operations he manages compared with the objectives and standards for these operations. The other members counsel with the leader to evaluate the work —expressing approval, identifying needs for improvement, and noting variances that affect others' performance. Through this activity, the regular meeting monitors and directs the organization's ongoing performance.

- *Recommendations.* The study of complex problems, decisions, and plans is usually done by technical staff or task forces (not at regular meetings). When their recommendations are brought to the regular meeting, the members are expected to accept, reject, or reassign the study after examining the work for accuracy, completeness, and practicability. Acceptance of the recommendation makes it the official line of action for the organization. Through this activity, the regular meeting initiates change.

- *News.* The members are expected to share any information that might present a threat or opportunity to the organization. News usually concerns actual or possible changes likely to affect at least two other members of the meeting. Such changes can usually be identified in a headline—thirteen words or less. The members are expected to scan this news and determine whether it merits some official response. Through this activity, regular meetings perform a learning function for the organization.

In all cases, regular meetings process information for the purpose of taking action. The meeting says "yes," "not yet," or "no." In some cases, what was once only an idea becomes an organizational reality backed by its resources. In other cases, efforts that have

---

[6]The term *pass down* has been borrowed from practices at Intel Corporation. In other organizations we have heard this type of agenda item referred to as *mandates* or *from on high.*

taken the resources of the organization for years may be brought to a decisive end. In all cases, its decisions are acts of official power.

Screen the Agenda before the Regular Meeting

To control the agenda, the leader must have a procedure by which at least all major items are screened before being presented to the meeting. The screening of these items may be done entirely by the meeting leader, or in the case of very complex regular meetings, by some specially appointed staff or standing committee.

Screening Criteria:

- Is it clear what action the meeting is expected to take? If not, obtain clarification.
- Is it a matter on which this regular meeting has the formal authority to act? If not, reroute it.
- Can it be dealt with initially or entirely at a lower level? If so, reroute it.
- Is this an item for a task force? If so, delegate it or bring it to the meeting for delegation.
- Does it concern at least three members of the meeting? If not, deal with it one-on-one.
- Is it thoroughly prepared?

    Is it appropriately documented?

    Has it been through all the prerequisite formal reviews?

    Has it been through appropriate informal review by members of the meeting?

    Are the next steps of implementation clearly specified?

    If the item fails to satisfy any of the above criteria, require the needed preparation.
- Given the time limits of the meeting, is it of high enough priority to be included on the agenda of this particular session? If not, postpone it to a later session.
- Does this item have an acceptable presenter? If not, appoint one. (It is not necessary for the sponsoring member to also be the presenter—a guest of the sponsoring member might be more appropriate. But the presenter should be identified prior to the meeting and approved by the leader.)

Every regular meeting should allow for emergency items. Such items often show up in that part of the meeting set aside for the news, or in a part of the agenda designated as open. But even in these cases, the members of the meeting ought to make sure their items fit the above criteria; and once the members of the meeting understand these surprise issues, the most appropriate action for the meeting is to delegate the matter rather than try to resolve it on the spur of the moment. This action and the screening procedure protects the organization from the uninformed exercise of its power.

Prepublish the Agenda

After the agenda has been screened it needs to be prepublished. This will allow the members to complete their preparation. A well-designed agenda will cover all the issues on this checklist:

_____ Name of the regular meeting

_____ Stop/start time for the meeting

_____ Place of meeting

_____ Meeting leader

_____ Name and title of the members

_____ Items for action

_____ Schedule for consideration of each item (start/stop times)

_____ Type of each item (pass down, status report, recommendation, news)

_____ Sponsor and presenter for each item (name and title of guest presenter, if appropriate)

_____ Special procedures for any item (e.g., FYI posters, case studies, etc.)

The prepublished agenda for regular meetings usually includes all the support documentation for each major item. All this should be sent to the members early enough to allow their proper preparation.[7]

Stay on the Agenda

Once the meeting begins, the leader needs to keep the group focused on its agenda:

- Get closure—decision and commissioning—on each item.
- For emergency items, get an accurate identification of the issue and an appropriate act of delegation.
- If inappropriate issues emerge—those that do not fit the screening criteria—get the issue off line (ask that the discussion be taken up outside the meeting).

Structuring the Permanent Membership

The second area of the leader's responsibility is to determine the permanent members of the regular meetings. Three rules will guide the leader in this process.

Rule 1: All the necessary officials should be permanent members. Once the authority of the regular meeting has been determined (its authority is usually the same as that of its formal leader), the next questions are the following:

1. What subfunctions (subordinates and staff) are most necessary in advising and implementing that authority?
2. Which subfunctions, by virtue of their representaion, will give the actions of the regular meeting appropriate symbolic power?

These officials (those responsible for these subfunctions) should be the *permanent members* of the regular meeting. (In this case,

---

[7]For another practical discussion of agenda publishing see pages 201-211 of *How to Make Meetings Work: The New Interaction* (4th Ed.) by Michael Doyle and David Straus, 1984, New York: Berkley.

we are calling the members "officials" because the decision to include them in the membership is more a matter of organizational position than it is a matter of personality. More about this appears in the discussion of Rule 2 below.) From time to time, other people in the organization will be invited to attend the regular meeting to help its members deal with specific issues; but it is the permanent members who are expected to exercise the regular meeting's power.

There seems to be no necessary restriction on the number of permanent members in regular meetings. Even spectators may be encouraged to attend as long as they are identified as a unique class of participants. It is more important to have all the right functionaries present than it is to achieve any particular size. As the permanent membership gets larger, the process will become more formal and attendance will become more symbolic than active. But these characteristics of the large regular meeting do not necessarily detract from its effectiveness—the large size may actually make the importance of its actions more apparent. On the other hand, a similar effect is sometimes achieved by having a very restricted permanent membership in a regular meeting where the proceedings are highly confidential.

Rule 2: Make the permanent membership of the meeting accurately mirror the formal structure of the organization. If the formal (official) structure of the organization makes distinctions among levels of authority, line and staff, employees and contractors, these distinctions should be reflected in the attendance and roles of the members in the regular meeting (see Figure 2). If some of the managers at one level are appointed, all their peers should be appointed, too. If some of one staff level are appointed, all the others of that level should be appointed.

**Organizational
Structure**   **Appropriate Structure
for Regular Meetings**

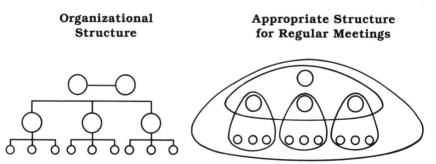

**Figure 2. Reflecting the Organizational Structure
in Regular Meetings**

Over time, managers often allow informal (operational) alterations in the formal structure that are not logical. They have difficulty following this rule about permanent membership and do not appreciate the significance of the problem they create. The following are some typical situations in which the formal structure does not make sense in light of actual operations:

- Certain staff members have assumed line authority;
- Certain subordinates have accepted responsibilities equal to or larger than that of the manager they supposedly report to and they now deal directly with their boss's boss;
- Certain functions that were once peer-like in size of responsibility have become unequal because of growth or reduction without the changes' being reflected in their managers' titles.

When a manager calls a regular meeting under these conditions, he tends to invite "anyone who wants to come" or "those I really need to talk to on a regular basis." The result is regular meetings in which the permanent membership confuses the image of the organization's formal distribution of authority. Figure 3 illustrates this confusion:

Staff or Line?   **Who Reports to Whom?**

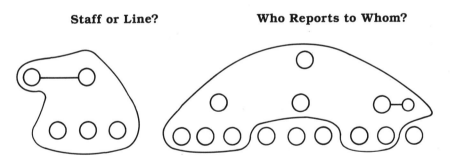

Figure 3. Confusions in Membership of Regular Meetings

Some managers try to justify these mistakes with superficial comments such as "I just invite anyone I need to talk to. After all, isn't that what meetings are all about—getting people together who need to communicate with each other? The way I see it, the more communication the better!"

The mistake, of course, reflects the manager's inability to keep the organization's tasks and human resources in harmony—to maintain fundamental justice in the distribution of work and its compensation. "Well, it's working for now, so let's not get too hung up in the little formalities," says the manager.

But the "little formalities" have a weight of thousands of years, and to ignore them has a consequence known for as long as human beings have been organized. At first the organization pays only the cost of stress—confused, frustrated employees who are inhibited by their own uncertainties. Then the resentment begins to grow, expressing itself in both unconscious and conscious withdrawal—the human assets stop caring, thinking, doing. The talented and self-confident go elsewhere; or if that is not possible they organize the resistance. The injustice of poor management cannot be dismissed as "little formalities."

Furthermore, organizational structure defines and legitimates power. Where the structure is permitted to be ambiguous, power will dissolve or become uncontrollable. Both outcomes are symptoms of dangerous organizational sickness.

Follow the rule: Make the membership of the regular meeting reflect the formal structure of the organization. Where this is awkward, confront the issue—formally restructure the organization.[8]

Rule 3: Attendance of permanent members is mandatory. Exceptions to this rule should be rare, always approved in advance, and always covered by a substitute approved by the meeting's leader. All the appropriate authorities must be present if the meeting is to exercise some part of the organization's formal power. Failure of the members to fulfill this responsibility should be seen as a formal disciplinary problem—insubordination or absence without leave.

Maintaining Appropriate Dynamics

To speak of *group dynamics* is to talk about the relative influence among the members of the group. Some members, through a variety of devices, achieve a dominant position, while others get pushed aside. The need for status is a psychological priority, and unless the leader gives it specific attention, the struggle for status continues underneath the stated purposes of the meeting, as a hidden agenda.

---

[8]For a full and technical discussion of integrated organizational and group structure, see pages 156-188 of *The Human Organization* (footnote 1).

In group work, the pecking order that emerges is the most important part of what is called a *norm state*. One way to represent a norm state is as a hill in a topographical map, as shown in Figure 4. The small ring in the center represents the top of the hill, the position of maximum influence; the outer rings represent lower levels of influence. The X's show how the members of the group are distributed on the hill of influence.

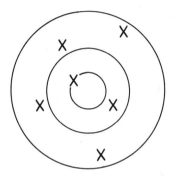

Figure 4. Typical Norm State of Poorly Led Meeting

Figure 4 shows a norm state typical of a poorly led meeting. The members are widely distributed throughout the influence structure. At least a few of the members are likely to be confused or uncertain about their role. Their efforts to get clarification will probably be seen as power plays and will initiate new struggles on the hidden agenda.

Much of the research on small groups focuses on the formation of norm states and how these affect the group's performance. Norm states are formed early in the life of the group, become surprisingly permanent as social structures, and largely determine the quality of the group's work.[9]

Special attention was given in the research to discovering the ideal norm state for group problem solving—the sort of work task

---

[9]For a general discussion of norm-state formation, see pages 31-38 of *Process Consultation: Its Role in Organization Development* by Edgar Schein, 1969, Reading, MA: Addison-Wesley; page 461 of *The Dynamics of Discussion: Communication in Small Groups* (2nd Ed.) by S. E. Jones, D. C. Barnlund, and F. S. Haiman, 1980, New York: Harper & Row; and pages 65-82 of *Organizational Culture and Leadership* by Edgar H. Schein, 1986, San Francisco: Jossey-Bass.

forces do. The best norm state for problem solving is an *equity* norm state as diagramed in Figure 5.

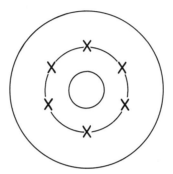

Figure 5. Norm State When All Members Have Equal Influence

In this norm state, all the members have an equal opportunity to influence the group's work; all the ideas and experiences of the members can flow toward understanding and resolving the problem.

To help a group achieve the equity norm state, leaders start the meeting with *inclusion activity*: anything that gets the members, including the leader, to act alike during the first few minutes of the meeting. Conformity of behavior at the beginning of the meeting sends out the message, especially on a nonverbal level, that all the members are equal. That message will strongly influence the formation of the group's norm state.

However, an equity norm state is not appropriate for most regular meetings. One of the functions of regular meetings is to reaffirm the organization's formal structure and its deliberately unequal distribution of authority among officials. Within any regular meeting it is very likely that at least two of these different levels of authority will be represented, and the joint action of these various authorities is the point of the meeting. To achieve this purpose, the regular meeting needs a norm state in which these levels and domains of authority are clearly distinguished. An informal, widely distributed, or equity norm state obscures these formal roles and diminishes the group's ability to act with authority. Role ambiguity and power do not mix well.

In a regular meeting between a manager and his or her immediate reports, it is appropriate that the norm state reflect the manager's superior authority. It might be diagramed as in Figure 6.

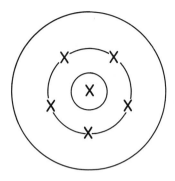

**Figure 6. Norm State Reflecting
Manager's Superior Authority**

In this norm state, the manager retains a clear position of dominance, and the peership of the direct reports is also confirmed. The manager's role represents the source of the group's authority; the manager may be influenced by the subordinates, but never actually overruled. If a last word is required, it should be perfectly clear that it will come from the manager. Furthermore, there should be little tolerance within the group for any bullying or power plays among the peers; all members are equally accountable to each other and the manager.

If more than one level of formal authority is included in a regular meeting, the norm state should reflect all the levels. Such a norm state is shown in Figure 7. Here is the appropriate norm state for a manager who holds a quarterly meeting with the two levels of managers immediately below him or her.

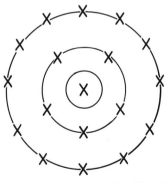

**Figure 7. Norm State Including More than
One Level of Authority**

Directing the formation of these complex norm states and maintaining them is one of the most important functions of the regular meeting leader. The method most useful for the accomplishment of this function will be called *recognition*.

Recognition

The meeting leader's best opportunity to form the proper norm state is during the first few minutes of the regular meeting—when the members of the group have the strongest need for social orientation. Even though the members may be doing their best to make a good impression, their nervous systems are hard at work trying to figure out the pecking order. It will probably take them at least twenty minutes, during which time they will not be able to focus well on anything else.

If the leader does not properly guide the members, the resulting norm state will probably not reflect the organization's formal structure or the roles the members are expected to play. The norm state will twist around the formal structure like elastic cords, constantly stressing and distorting the meeting's performance.

Every time a group comes together, even one that has been meeting for years, it spends the first few minutes working the hidden agenda again. The leader should see this as an opportunity! This is the time to shape the norm state to support the roles members are expected to play.

The leader exerts control by starting the regular meeting with *recognition*. Recognition draws attention to the *formal relationships* the members have with each other. It reminds the members that in this setting they are not just individual human beings, they are functionaries—with specific roles within the organization's power structure.

Remember that recognition will have to be given at the beginning of every meeting. The message has to be communicated consistently at all levels: visually and audibly as well as cognitively. The leader cannot give a lecture each time! So, as a leader, think about this with your eyes: How can you make the roles of your members visible during the first minutes of the meeting? Then think about this with your ears: How can you make the roles of your members audible during the first minutes of the meeting?

It is entirely appropriate, for instance, to begin regular meetings emphasizing the differences in roles through roll calls, seating arrangements, and reminders of the rules about when participants can speak and what subjects they can address. The opening of the meeting should be a process that draws attention to roles and functions rather than the individual persons fulfilling them, and the process should show the *intended* relations between those roles rather than any modifications that may have evolved informally. (Lists of suggestions appear on under "Recognition Possibilities" in Part 3.)

For models, think about the ceremonial aspects of courtrooms, Congressional hearings, and military briefings. Probably your visual and auditory cues should be less powerful than these examples, but to ignore the cues altogether sends out a message that your meeting is unimportant. Then, remember how your meeting starts now: In what order do the members arrive? How do they dress? Where do they sit? Who usually speaks first? You may discover that the foundation for recognition has already been laid. If the foundation is appropriate, build on it.

For many managers, formalities and deliberate attention to status are offensive. They see this as a throwback to more traditional forms of organization. They say, "I don't want a 'formal' organization; I want everyone relaxed and friendly."

An organizational culture in which everyone is friendly and approachable is a definite asset. Structure and role clarity are essential to perpetuating such a culture because respect and affection among people at work is built on clear and successful role performance. Furthermore, this culture is supported not by an absence of structure but by a more complex structure—a flatter hierarchy interlaced with many matrices. To sustain such a structure, even greater effort must be spent in role affirmation. Effective regular meetings are a primary means of accomplishing this, and a greater number of them are required to maintain a relaxed and friendly culture.

In the not-so-distant past, all organizations displayed their formal structure and authorities in a pageantry of procession and costume. Such extremes may no longer be necessary or appropriate; but if there is ever a time and place for formality in an organization's culture, it is the first few minutes of its regular meetings. As organizations grow ever larger and more complex, this moment of formality may become an important way of maintaining role clarity.

Guiding the Process

Group *dynamics* deals with the issues of social status and roles. Group *process* focuses on the procedures by which the group handles its task.

The leader must move the group, thoroughly and without confusion, through the task at hand. There are many procedures to help accomplish this goal, and the second part of this book describes several of the most useful. But behind all of the procedures lies one basic process (see Figure 8). It is important for the leader to understand this basic process and to make sure the group follows it. Central to the process is decision making. Decisions are the regular meeting's acts of power. The kinds of decisions that the group can make and the level of agreement expected are the most important things for the leader to know and use when guiding the process.

Once leaders are thoroughly familiar with the basic process and its decisional elements, they can further help their regular meetings get their work done by the selection of appropriate procedures.

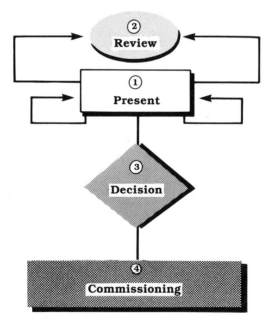

Figure 8. The Basic Process for Regular Meetings

Once again, the basic process for regular meetings is quite different from the one used by task forces. Task forces use a three-part process that begins with building a common information base, proceeds through a second phase of interpretation, and finally, in a third phase, achieves resolution. Participation in the process is highly cognitive as it drives with a sort of mental ruthlessness toward the most intelligent resolution possible.

Regular meetings also require intelligent participation, but *their purpose is to validate rather than generate ideas—to authorize rather than discover—to act rather than contemplate.* This unique function is performed with a different, four-part process that the regular meeting applies to every agenda item. The four parts of the process are *presentation, review, decision,* and *commissioning.*

Presentation. This is the initial statement of the agenda item. The person making this statement is the *presenter* and may be the meeting's leader, any permanent member, or an invited expert. This statement may be accompanied with documentation and audio-visual aids. It should at least provide the following information:

- Definition of the agenda item (pass down, operations report, recommendation, or news);
- Action expected from the regular meeting;
- Brief description of the most important elements of the item; and
- An invitation to begin the review.

Review. This is the act of examining a report or recommendation—testing its intellectual, operational, and political validity—and judging whether the action is aligned with the organization's mission and values. This is usually the longest part of the process.

Done well, the discussion is restricted to reviewing previous thinking. It does not duplicate the cognitive work of staff experts or task forces. The previous thinking of the experts or task forces, should it withstand the regular meeting's review, will become the organization's official explanation of its action.

Decision. Based on the outcome of the review, members of the regular meeting make a decision. They decide that all is well—that the status quo will prevail—or they declare their intention to do something new or to stop doing something. Sometimes they decide only that they will continue to consider the matter.

This phase of the process is relatively brief, but it is the act of power, the point of the regular meeting, and in some cases it should have the force of dramatic climax.

Commissioning. The decision is followed by checking to make sure everyone understands its implications. Commissioning checks to see that all the members are aligned to support the action. This step is especially important when the review discussion reveals that some members have strong disagreement with the course of action finally determined. (See "Levels of Agreement" below.)

Commissioning is not full-scale action planning—usually that has already been done as part of the report or recommendation. But if action planning has not been done, the commissioning may be the act of delegating this task.

It should be clear that very little original thinking occurs during regular meetings. The issues and recommendations have been thoroughly explored prior to the meeting. Usually this prior exploration has been shared more or less privately with all the members of the regular meeting before the item is placed on the agenda. During these private sessions, the members may have made suggestions or expressed objections that have influenced the form of the recommendation. As a result, regular meetings can have a feeling of *going through the motions.*

All this is entirely appropriate. An effective regular meeting takes what has been found to be a highly intelligent, proper answer and then confirms and empowers it as the organization's official solution. Regular meetings have the unique ability to transform ideas into social reality, expressing them in terms of the organization's money, land, buildings, equipment, supplies, human energy, and reputation. This transformation of ideas is a major accomplishment. When a regular meeting can do this with the ease of a drama troupe performing a familiar play, things are going well!

Decision Options for Regular Meetings

The function of the regular meeting is to act—to decide. No matter what the regular meeting is responding to—pass downs, evaluating operations, considering recommendations, or listening to the news—in all cases it should get to the decision phase of its process for each item of the agenda. There are essentially only three decisions that can be made:

Approve/Disapprove. The regular meeting determines that a performance or recommendation is acceptable, or that it is unacceptable and must be corrected or stopped. This is the most fundamental and conclusive of the decision options and should be seen as the most desirable. Any time this option is avoided or delayed, it is a sign that items are coming onto the agenda less than fully prepared.

Delegation. Whether the regular meeting *approves* or *disapproves*, it may also follow its decision with an act of delegation. If so, it appoints a person or a task force to implement its decision.

For each task delegated, at least one permanent member of the meeting needs to be designated as a sponsor. This member may in turn delegate the task to someone else but will still be the accountable link to the regular meeting.

A complete act of delegation includes all the following directives:

- Clear statement of the result expected from the assignment;
- The regular meeting's sponsor for the assignment;
- Whether or not the sponsor is to act alone or form a task force;
- The sponsor's authority to act (which would take one of the following forms):

   Act but do not report;

   Act and report immediately what was done;

   Act and report through regular reporting cycles;

   Do not act but evaluate the situation and make a recommendation.

- The deadline for accomplishing the assignment.

When the act of delegation involves establishing a task force, the statement of the directives listed above becomes the *charter* of the task force. It is important that a task force understand its charter and recognize when it is moving away from it. Moving beyond the original charter is a very common and even natural occurrence. As the task force becomes involved in its task, it learns of factors and alternatives not known to the regular meeting that established the charter. An entirely different definition of the problem or a wholly new method of solution may be discovered. When this happens it is appropriate for the task force to keep the sponsor informed. The sponsor must determine whether to make a progress report to the regular meeting and to seek a redefinition of the charter.

Tabling. The regular meeting may decide that a recommendation is basically acceptable, but that the action should be postponed to some indefinite time, so it tables the idea. It may also table the discussion of an issue that is not of high enough priority at the moment. When a matter is tabled, the implication is that the regular meeting recognizes its relevance and intends to pick up the issue again at a later time. Tabling should be seen as a commitment to commit at a later time. The leader should not allow the regular meeting to confuse tabling with an act of disapproval—as a soft way of rejecting ideas.

Tabling is an act of receiving information and keeping it in one's peripheral vision until it is needed. This is often the only appropriate response to the news. Nevertheless, tabling is the least decisive of the four forms of resolution and should be used sparingly.

Levels of Agreement

Resolution in regular meetings does not necessarily mean that all the members are in agreement. Members are often required to commit to actions about which they have expressed doubts. Regular meetings can act with a variety of levels of agreement:

Unanimous Consent. When total agreement is required, the decision-making process is technically called *unanimous consent.* Every member has veto power over the group's decision—if any one member disagrees, no action is taken and the status quo reigns. This works in some task forces, but it is rarely practical for regular meetings. The process requires too much time, invites intense conflict, and often mires the organization in the status quo. Furthermore, consensus implies that all the members of the group are peers in authority, so the process might obscure the organization's structures.

Voting. Majority rule might be appropriate for regular meetings in which the members are delegates of constituencies that are equal in status. Such meetings are clearly political in nature and should be so without apology. A rational resolution of the conflicts among such constituencies is often not possible, and voting is preferable to open warfare. Assuming the compliance of the minority, voting preserves both the meeting's ability to act and the resources and issues of its minority. But voting is a process almost always distorted by power play. In the regular meetings of managers, a more rational process is desirable.

Voting also denies that any member, including the leader, has any superior authority. The denial of the leader's superior authority is a total contradiction of the assumptions of hierarchy. Unless the leader's vote is given some unique and superior empowerment, voting is inappropriate as a decision-making method in a hierarchical organization.

Consultative Consensus. In this process it is clear from the start that the decision will be made by only one member of the group. In regular meetings where the members are part of a hierarchical management structure, the decision maker ought to be the highest-ranking official—usually the formal leader of the meeting. In this way, the process displays a distribution of authority consistent with the organization's structure.

The other members offer their advice to enrich the leader's understanding of the issue. Through the group process the leader gets the members' advice, their help in evaluating one another's advice, and a sense of the meeting. With this information the leader decides.

Though it is possible for the leader to act against the advice of all the other members, consultative decision making is not necessarily autocratic. Whether or not the process becomes autocratic depends on the listening skills of the leader and the effectiveness of the members as consultants. Well led, consultative consensus is the primary instrument of participative management. It provides the necessary structure for each member's effort to influence the decision-making process.

Sometimes, the decision maker will be surprised or confused by the consultative discussion. It may be wise to table the decision until the decision maker has had time to validate certain opinions and reflect on the discussion. If such a delay occurs, the leader should reconvene the consulting group and announce the decision to them first. At that time, the leader should invite further questioning until the members understand how their arguments were evaluated and the decision finally made. In this way, the consultative process educates all members sufficiently to make them reliable representatives of the official point of view. This is important, because when the decision is announced, all the members are expected to support it regardless of whether they agree. In some cases, the members will find themselves in a position described as "disagree and commit."[10]

---

[10]For an excellent though different analysis of group decision making, see pages 52-57 of *Process Consultation: Its role in Organization Development* by Edgar Schein, 1969, Reading, MA: Addison-Wesley.

Selecting Appropriate Procedures

Though there is one basic process for regular meetings (presentation, review, decision, and commissioning), there are a variety of procedures to facilitate this process. A number of them are outlined in the next section of the book. Figure 9 can be used in selecting among them.

Agenda Type

Procedures	Pass Downs	Status Reviews	Recommendations	News
Agenda Building				■
Bin Listing	■	■	■	
Expected Responses	★	★	★	★
Case Studies	■			■
Performance Plan Review		■		
Operations Review		■		
Leaders's Plan Update		■		
Recommendations Review	■		■	
Start/Stop/Alert				■
Highlights/Lowlights				■
FYI Posters				■
For the Good of the Order				■
Problem Definition Procedures		■	■	■
Assignment Matrix	■	■	■	■
Flea Market				■
+/− Meeting Evaluation				

The " ■ " symbol shows which procedures are best for each agenda type. The " ★ " symbol has been used to recommend that Expected Responses be required as part of the presentation for each agenda item.

Figure 9. Guide for Selecting Appropriate Procedures

Providing a Memory System

Memory systems must serve two purposes for regular meetings:

1. Facilitate the meeting's discussion.
2. Make a permanent, official record of the actions taken.

Facilitating the Discussion

To facilitate discussion, the leader needs to make sure that all members of the meeting have copies of the documentation for each important item on the agenda. This is especially true where details such as production statistics and financial data are involved. Copies of any last-minute additions or corrections should be provided, too. In addition, the presenter for each item should be encouraged to use charts or overhead transparencies to guide discussion.

While it is not usually necessary to make a running record of everything said during regular meetings, it is a good idea to have a flip chart and markers ready for recording the modifications and final decisions made on all important items. Displaying this before the group during its meeting assures accuracy and will help the group get through the commissioning part of the process.

Making the Permanent, Official Record

Since the actions of the regular meeting are official in nature, minutes should be maintained that at least record the decisions made. The minutes may be as informal as the leader's handwritten notes, but often a more official set should be maintained and occasionally reviewed for accuracy by the members.

In addition to the official minutes, some actions of regular meetings should be remembered symbolically. Possible symbols include letters and certificates of recognition, plaques, trophies, T-shirts, photographs, and historic memorabilia. During meeting preparation, the leader should review the agenda for appropriate opportunities to brighten the meeting's announcements with such symbols.[11]

PARTICIPATING IN REGULAR MEETINGS

These responsibilities will be discussed under three headings: attitudes, participant skills, and critical-thinking skills.

Attitudes

It is necessary to talk about attitudes first, because the specific behaviors required of each member will be too diverse to predict. We can say that the behaviors will be situationally relevant expressions of three attitudes:

1. *Act from your formal role, not just your personality.* In regular meetings you are part of the display of the organization's structure and system of authority. You are a symbol of a part of that system; so are your fellow members. How you treat each other in the meeting is not just a matter of human interaction; it is also a representation of how the various parts of the organization relate to each other. Your actions should be an accurate and respectful reflection of those roles you play.

2. *Act as though you were responsible for* all *the functions represented.* When you are alone, your authority and responsibility are limited to your department. But when you attend a regular meeting, you share in the authority of that meeting's leader. You are not just a representative of your function, you are a resource on loan to the meeting's leader for use in managing all the represented functions. Think of yourself as a consultant to the meeting leader.

3. *When the meeting starts, be ready.* Tardiness or failure to have done one's preparation delivers a message: the function you

---

[11]For an expanded discussion of group memory and the skills for being a recorder, see pages 38-54 and 125-142 of *How to Make Meetings Work* (footnote 7).

represent is careless and out of control. Understand that in this set-ting these behaviors not only offend the other members personally, they also disgrace the organization.

Participant Skills

The members of regular meetings need to have all the basic skills of group participation. These skills can be grouped as task-related skills and maintenance related-skills.[12]

Task-Related Skills:
To Help the Group Process Its Information

The following are task-related skills:

Initiating. Someone gets the ball rolling both at the beginning and at critical transitions of the meeting.

Providing Information and Opinions. Everyone comes prepared to offer relevant information and has a sense of obligation to do so.

Asking for Information and Opinions. This is especially impor-tant for pointing out omissions in the data base.

Clarifying. Restating a point to make sure it is understood.

Elaborating. The ability to see the implications of an idea and add examples to emphasize a point.

Summarizing. Stating what has been accomplished so far in a way that also focuses on where the group is in its procedures and looks toward next steps.

---

[12]The classification of role functions in a group was presented in "The Effects of Cooperation and Competition upon Group Process" by M. Deutsch, *Group Dynamics—Research and Theory* (2nd Ed.) by D. Cartwright and A. Zander (Eds.), 1960, Evanston, IL: Row Peterson. See also "Functional Roles of Group Members" by K. Benne and P. Sheats, 1948, *Journal of Social Issues, 2,* pp. 42-47, and "A Set of Categories for the Analysis of Small Group Interaction" by R. F. Bales, 1950, *American Sociological Review, 15,* pp. 257-263.

Compromising. Finding a rational unity between conflicting ideas.

Maintenance Skills: To Keep a Group's Dynamics Properly Balanced

The following are maintenance skills:

Gatekeeping. Inviting a silent member to speak or turning attention away from one who talks too much.

Harmonizing. The ability to calm others and relieve them of emotions that start getting in the way of good thinking.

Testing the Group's Norm State. Calling direct attention to behaviors that seem to distort the group's proper norm state. Be careful! First try this skill with the meeting leader in private.

Encouraging. Helping the group deal with frustration and low morale, sometimes by recalling past successes.

Critical-Thinking Skills

The members of regular meetings need to be especially good at critical thinking. During the review phase, the members must listen and question to make sure that reports and recommendations have been carefully done.

No one can be an expert in everything; that is why the regular meeting delegates work to experts and task forces. But how can the members judge the quality of this expert work so they can be accountable for its enactment? The check list in Figure 10 will help make the judgment.

When performing the review, a regular meeting is testing the quality of the work already done. If in the process it appears that there are weaknesses in the work, they should be noted, but *the regular meeting should not attempt to do the work over.* Unless the corrections are very simple, the error should simply be noted and then taken into consideration when the final decision is made. If the errors so weaken the work that it cannot be relied on as a basis for action, the recommendation is redelegated or rejected. Otherwise, the regular meeting will accept the recommendation.

Examining the database:

Clarity
Readable formats
Sources understood
Time frames compatible
Definitions clear and consistent

Validity
Data collection procedure
Bias free
Error free
All appropriate sources consulted

Constraints
Limits of data clear
Limits appropriate

Examining the interpretation of the data:

Alternatives considered

Assumptions of favored alternative
Problem definition/original thesis
Criteria used for evaluation
Priority of various criteria
Effects of history, tradition, policy

Positive and negative consequences of favored alternative
Comparative consequences of other alternatives
Assumed probabilities of consequences

Examining the conclusion or recommendation:

Conclusion "in a nutshell"

Changes required
Organizational mission or values
Policy
Structure
Leadership
Methods or procedures
Who is affected

How implemented
Schedule
Resources required
Who is accountable

Figure 10. Recommendations Review Check List

Reviews should be done with intellectual rigor. But remember that this intensity of critical thinking by people who hold significant positions of power can often intimidate the presenter. If this intimidation causes presenters to perform at less than their best, it does not serve the organization well. So review the work thoroughly, respectfully, and perhaps gently, in the spirit of a cooperative search for understanding. Make your final decision on behalf of the organization, not the feelings of any individual.

Part 2:
Procedures

➡ AGENDA BUILDING[13]

When to Use This Procedure

1. When you begin a discussion of current issues, none of which is on the prepublished meeting agenda—to organize the "open agenda" part of a meeting;
2. When you need to preview the issues people want to address in open discussion;
3. When you want to prioritize issues to make the best use of limited time.

Materials Needed

1. Flip chart.
2. Felt-tipped markers.
3. Masking tape.

How to Use This Procedure

1. The leader lists on the flip chart all issues members would like to bring to the attention of the group.
2. The leader sorts issues into those the group can deal with immediately and those for later action. This set of categories may be useful:

---

[13]There are many procedures for agenda building. For another alternative see page 91 of *How to Make Regular Meetings Work* (footnote 7).

Here & Now—To be resolved in this meeting.

Next Meeting—To be resolved by this group in a future meeting.

Assignment—To be assigned to one group member who will resolve the issue and report back in a future meeting.

Task Force—To be resolved by a group especially appointed to deal with this one issue (not necessarily by this same group).

The leader codes each item to indicate how the group decides to categorize the issues. For instance, "now" can be written next to each item for this meeting; "next," "assign," or "TF," beside the other items.

3. The leader determines the sequence in which the here-and-now items will be discussed and leads the discussion of these items. Time must be reserved for the remaining steps.

4. The leader assigns presenters, if appropriate, for those issues the group has decided to deal with in its future meetings.

5. The leader appoints a member to assume responsibility for those items designated as assignments.

6. The leader chooses a group member to sponsor each task force, and perhaps determines what other experts should be on the force (this may be left to the sponsor).

Notes

1. The leader may want to do the assignment Steps 4 to 6 before discussing the here-and-now issues. If so, be prepared to repeat Steps 4 to 6 if you run out of time or discover other issues during the discussion.

2. The assignment matrix procedure may be helpful for Steps 4 to 6.

AGENDA BUILDING
In a Nutshell

1. List issues.
2. Sort issues:
   Now
   Next
   Assignment
   Task Force
3. Prioritize "now" issues and discuss.
4. Assign future presenters for "next" issues.
5. Delegate "assignment" issues.
6. Appoint sponsor and perhaps members for "task-force" issues.

BIN LIST[14]

When to Use This Procedure

1. When the group has come up with a lot of issues, some of which need to be put aside until later;
2. When you want to keep the group focused on its current task and other agendas come up.

Materials Needed

1. Flip chart.
2. Felt-tipped markers.

How to Use This Procedure

1. Ahead of time, or when issues come up that cannot be addressed immediately, the leader labels a fresh page of the flip chart, "Bin List."
2. The leader explains that the bin list is for issues that the group will remember to deal with later, perhaps at the end of the planned portion of the meeting.
3. The leader hangs the bin list on the wall in an out-of-the-way but visible place.
4. The leader adds distracting issues to the bin list as they occur.
5. The leader deals with the issues on the bin list when the group has time.

---

[14]This procedure is often used at Intel Corporation. It is sometimes called "flag listing" in other organizations.

Notes

The "Agenda Building" procedure or "Assignment Matrix" procedure can be used to deal with items on the bin list. To do this, leave time at the end of the meeting.

BIN LIST
In A Nutshell

1. Label flip chart: "Bin List."
2. Explain: a list of items for later.
3. Hang chart on a side wall.
4. Add items as distractions occur.
5. Deal with items at appropriate time.

➡ EXPECTED RESPONSE

When to Use This Procedure

1. When you announce an issue for discussion or an item on your agenda;
2. When you want to intensify the listening and questioning activity of the group;
3. When you want to limit debate on "news" items.

Materials Needed

None.

How to Use This Procedure

1. The leader asks each presenter of an agenda item to indicate what response is expected from the group. One of these responses should be indicated:

   Approve/Disapprove. The group is expected to authorize the report or recommendation as officially acceptable or as the official course of action to which the organization is committed.

   Delegate. The group is expected to determine whether the issue merits further inquiry or action by assigning it to one of its members or by appointing one of its members as a sponsor for a task force.

   Table/Be Advised. The group is not expected to take action at this time, but needs to know the issues and be ready to deal with them should they emerge later.

2. The leader leads a group discussion to achieve the response desired and summarizes the discussion by checking with the presenter or group to make sure the desired response has been given before moving to any other item.

Notes

Tabling is the least demanding of all responses. Items presented for this response get the least motivated attention. (Several such issues in a row make for a rather dull meeting.) As leader, invest the group with the greater authority of the other responses (approve/disapprove and delegate) and encourage the other presenters to do the same.

EXPECTED RESPONSE
In a Nutshell

1. Presenter says what response is expected in presentation:
   Approval/Disapproval
   Delegate
     Individual
     Task Force
   Table/Be Advised

2. Presenter and leader conduct discussion:
   Review
   Decision
   Commissioning

➡ CASE STUDIES

When to Use This Procedure

1. When an informational item has important implications that may not be readily perceived by the other members of the group, or which has apparently been ignored by the group in the past;
2. When you want to provoke discussion.

Materials Needed

1. The presenter for the item brings a prepared case.

How to Use This Procedure

1. The presenter brings written copies of the informational item and one or more written cases to which the information must be applied.

   EXAMPLE:

   > *Pass Down.* In the performance plans for next quarter, managers should only address results expected from the performance of their employees. No manager's plan should include "supervisory" activities. This is consistent with the assumption that the only way to evaluate the effectiveness of supervisory activity is on the basis of the results such activity achieves *through others.*
   >
   > If you understand this directive, you should recognize that only four activities from the following list are appropriate subjects for a manager's performance plan:

    a. 100 percent on-time performance appraisals.

    b. Number of work improvement discussions with employees.

    c. Reduction of errors in public reports.

    d. Systematic conducting of staff meetings.

    e. Efforts at resolution of intrastaff conflict.

    f. Reduced through-put time for staff work.

    g. Training in customer relations.

    h. Reduced customer complaints about rudeness.

    i. Implementation of new project planning system.

    j. Delivery of all project outputs on deadline.

2. The presenter makes a report and directs the members of the group to work alone on the case study.

3. The presenter announces the answers and conducts a discussion for further clarification.

Notes

1. This procedure is largely a means to accomplish commissioning. A decision is made and then time is spent making sure all members understand the implications for their follow-through. Understanding this, leaders and presenters will find frequent use for the procedure.

2. For the curious, the appropriate subjects for a manager's performance plan are c, f, h, and j.

CASE STUDIES
In a Nutshell

1. Presenter brings informational item and case study/studies.

2. Members work the case(s) alone.

3. Presenter announces answers and conducts discussion.

➡ PERFORMANCE-PLAN REVIEW[15]

When to Use This Procedure

1. During quarterly, semiannual, or annual review of the members' performance plans—the standards and objectives they are intending to achieve during the next planning period;
2. To increase:

   The significance of status reporting.

   The importance and quality of goal setting.

   Operational cooperation among the members.

   The likelihood of goal achievement.

   The authority of your staff as a team.

Materials Needed

1. Each member must bring his or her performance plan for the next planning period. These plans are usually discussed with the staff leader before being brought before the regular meeting.

How to Use This Procedure

At the Beginning of the Planning Period:

1. Each member takes a turn presenting his or her objectives to the other members of the staff.

---

[15]This procedure is adapted from one used at Intel Corporation. It also draws on the author's work with the training program, "Performance Planning and Appraisal."

2. In a consultative mode to the reporting member and meeting leader, the other members evaluate the appropriateness of the objectives, their measures, and their priority. The following check list may help guide the discussion:

   a. Does the plan address results rather than process?

   b. Is the plan simple enough to promote focus of attention and resources?

   c. Does it address the key results—the heart of the department's/performer's function?

   d. Are both the pace (schedule) of the performance and the quality of the results described in measurable terms?

   e. Are the pace and measures both appropriate and realistic? Is the level of performance sufficient? Are the results achievable? Are resources sufficient to support the plan? Is the information available to validate the measures?

   f. Are the priorities appropriate?

3. All members of the staff specifically explore where the performance plans connote cooperation and clarify one another's roles when appropriate.

4. At the conclusion of each plan's discussion, the meeting leader presents a summary, giving special attention to any changes to be made and specifically assigning responsibility to the reporting member for making and presenting the revisions in the next regular meeting.

5. The meeting leader may either present his or her performance plan first or build it during the meeting by picking up objectives from the members.

At the End of the Planning Period:

1. Each member brings a self-rated performance plan and provides a summary report of his or her department's actual performance with explanation of variances. Where problems occurred, the reporting member should describe the corrective actions taken. Where the plans were exceeded, the reporting member should explain the causes.

2. In a consultative mode to the reporting member and meeting leader, the members of the meeting question the performance report and confirm or recommend changing the rating.

3. At the end of each performance report, the leader summarizes the rating and comments as appropriate.

Notes

1. This process shares the leader's authority with the staff, but it does not transfer full authority to the group. By keeping the group in the consultative mode, the leader clearly retains final authority.
2. This process can be shortened by limiting presentations to the highest priority objectives of each individual or to the leader's objectives (assuming that each staff member has responsibility for at least one of these objectives).

PERFORMANCE-PLAN REVIEW
In a Nutshell

At Beginning of Planning Period:

1. Each member presents objectives.
2. Other members consult with presenter and leader:
   a. Results *vs.* process
   b. Simple; focused
   c. Key results—heart of presenter's function
   d. Measures for pace and quality
   e. Measures realistic:
      Level of performance sufficient
      Achievable
      Sufficient resources
      Information available on measures
   f. Priorities appropriate
3. Explore needs for cooperation and identify roles.
4. Leader summarizes and delegates changes.
5. Leader presents own plan, first or as summary.

At the End of the Planning Period:

1. Each member presents self-rated performance plan and summary of variances and actions taken.
2. Members discuss report and recommend rate.
3. Leader summarizes discussion and rate.

⮕ **OPERATIONS REVIEW**

When to Use This Procedure

1. At the regular meeting where the current period of operational performance is to be reviewed (last day, week, month);
2. When you want to:
   - Increase attention to good performance;
   - Get group help in identifying problem areas;
   - Increase the resources focused on problem solving;
   - Encourage operational cooperation;
   - Increase the authority of the regular meeting.

Materials Needed

1. Flip chart.
2. Felt-tipped markers.

Each reporting member provides the meeting with copies of his or her operations report. (Within the format of these reports, the standards and objectives applicable to the current period of performance should be provided. See Note 1 below.)

How to Use This Procedure

1. The reporting member briefly describes the status of his or her operations in reference to the standards and objectives that apply. All variances are highlighted. Where problems occurred, the reporting member should describe the corrective actions taken. Where the plans were exceeded, the reporting member should explain the causes.

2. In a consultative mode to the reporting member and meeting leader, the members of the meeting question the performance report acknowledging successes and confirming or advising on the corrective actions.

  (Beware of becoming involved in complex problem solving. In some cases, making assignments or establishing task forces will be appropriate.)

3. At the end of each report, the leader announces the decision (approval or disapproval and required corrective action) and takes time to make sure everyone understands the implications of the decision (commissioning).

Notes

1. One option is to do only Step 1 with all the reporting members, listing on a flip chart at the end of each report the significant exceptions to which the meeting will give its attention later. This is a form of agenda building and allows the group to survey all the operational issues, prioritize and combine them before moving to Steps 2 and 3.

2. Sometimes it is not necessary to hear all the members' operational reports at the same meeting. Various schedules of reporting allow the meeting to deal with some departments at one meeting and other departments at another.

3. If this procedure is used in relationship to any one member's operations, all those who are his or her peers within the meeting should also be required to report at one time or another.

4. Note the comment above (at Materials Needed) on providing the member's standards and objectives. Without these, status reports will only be *news*. To make an evaluative judgment the members must know not only what was done, but what was expected. It is this comparative feature of status reports that make them meaningful and stimulating.

OPERATIONS REVIEW
In a Nutshell

1. Each member reports status of current operations:

   Actual performance
   Variances from goals or standards
   Corrective actions taken
   Causes for excellence

2. Other members consult with presenter and leader concerning performance issues and appropriate actions.

3. Leader summarizes.

Option:

After each report (Step 1), identify issues only, prioritize and discuss all performance issues after all reports have been made.

➡ *LEADER'S PLAN UPDATE*[16]

When to Use This Procedure

1. At the regular meeting in which the current period of operational performance is to be reviewed (last day, week, month);
2. When you want to:
    - Increase attention to good performance;
    - Get group help in identifying problem areas;
    - Increase the resources focused on problem solving;
    - Encourage operational cooperation (see Note 2 below);
    - Increase the authority of the regular meeting.

Materials Needed

1. Flip chart.
2. Felt-tipped markers.
3. The meeting leader's performance plan.

How to Use This Procedure

1. The leader displays his or her performance plan (quarterly or annual) as a series of objectives or standards, each one stated at the top of a separate sheet of flip-chart paper. These are hung on the walls of the meeting room prior to the beginning of the meeting. (It is assumed that the leader's performance plan is an expression of the key results expected from the parts of the organization managed by the members of the meeting.)

---

[16]The procedure is adapted from the practice of Gwen McDonald, Personnel Director for the City of Oakland, California.

2. The leader calls attention to the charts. (If this procedure is being used for the first time, some explanation of each objective or standard statement may be appropriate.) Any additions, deletions, or modifications (if any) to the performance plan are highlighted. Finally the leader defines the period of time (last day, week, or month) on which members are to report.

3. The leader provides ten to fifteen minutes for the group members to mark on each appropriate chart what has been accomplished during the reporting period to support the objective or standard stated at the top. All members work at this simultaneously. (See Note 1 below.)

4. Group members, seated or standing where all can see the charts, elaborate verbally on the notes just made. Verbal reports may be made in priority order of the objectives, chart by chart; or members—one at a time—may be asked to report all contributions to the leader's performance plan. The focus of the meeting is usually best under the first option—chart by chart.

5. As the verbal reports are made, all members question one another to make sure the accomplishments are clear or that performance weaknesses are identified. Occasionally this discussion will require more notes be added to the charts. The discussion is only for clarification—no corrective action should be taken until the group's performance on the entire plan has been previewed.

6. The leader summarizes the discussion from Steps 4 and 5, highlighting which performances are commendable, and inviting elaboration on these commendations from other members of the group.

7. The leader also highlights which performances require corrective action. These issues are then written on a "problems chart."

8. The leader conducts discussion on each item listed on the problems chart. Each problem is identified (see "Problem Definition" procedure) and if simple enough is solved immediately. Otherwise, once the problem has been tentatively defined, the group determines who will be responsible for its solution through an act of delegation. (The "Assignment Matrix" procedure will be helpful.)

9. The leader summarizes the discussion of performance-plan accomplishments.

Notes

1. Allowing time for the notes to be made during the meeting (as suggested in Step 3 of "How to Use This Procedure") provides a shift-of-energy activity. But some leaders may prefer to have the members add these notes to the charts during the last few minutes before the meeting begins.
2. This procedure is especially helpful in emphasizing teamwork. It reinforces the perception that the leader's performance is in fact the sum of the performances of his or her subordinates, and that the subordinates are team members in the accomplishment of the overall plan.
3. This procedure can be used for status review of project teams. In that case, the project's chart is used instead of the leader's plan.

LEADER'S PLAN UPDATE
In a Nutshell

1. Leader displays plan on flip chart.
2. Leader:

    Introduces plan;

    Explains any alterations;

    Defines reporting period (last day, week, month).
3. All members simultaneously make notes on the appropriate charts about their contributions to the objective or standard stated at the top of the chart.
4. Group members verbally explain their notes.
5. Discussion for clarification is conducted.
6. Commendable performance is recognized.

7. Needs for corrective action are listed on a problem chart.

8. Each item on the problem chart is resolved or delegated.

9. Leader summarizes discussion.

➡ RECOMMENDATIONS REVIEW

When to Use This Procedure

1. When a delegated task force comes back to the regular meeting to seek ratification of its recommendations;
2. When contractors, consultants, or vendors bring proposals for approval to the regular meeting;
3. When some proposal or recommendation is presented as a pass down from some higher center of authority in order for members of the regular meeting to review it and give advice before higher-level action is taken.

Materials Needed

1. A copy of the supporting documentation for each member of the meeting.

How to Use This Procedure

1. The presenter for the recommendation is introduced either by the leader or the sponsor. Sufficient information should be given to assist the members in understanding the expertise and organizational role(s) of the presenter.
2. The presenter makes an initial presentation that should include a statement of the response expected from the meeting (see "Expected Response" procedure), a clear statement of the recommendation, and any preliminary comments about the process behind the recommendation that seem appropriate. This presentation will often include audiovisual aids and other documentation.

3. In a consultative mode to the leader of the meeting, the members question the process behind the recommendation and the implications of the recommendation until satisfied that sufficient information has been provided to make a decision. (See Note 1 below. Also the Reviewing Recommendations Check List at the end of this procedure can assist members in this questioning.)

4. The leader thanks the presenter and asks him or her to audit the following discussion. The leader then asks the members of the reviewing group whether or not they would advise the leader to accept the recommendation, and this discussion continues until the leader is ready to decide.

5. The leader of the meeting summarizes the discussion and announces what action will be taken.

6. As part of the commissioning, the leader usually names those who will be involved in the next steps (if next steps are to be taken) and thanks the sponsor and presenter for their contributions.

Notes

1. A carefully prepared recommendation comes from some form of the following process:

   • Collection and study of information regarding the issue;
   • Determination of alternatives;
   • Selection of best alternative.

   To approve the recommendation, the regular meeting has to review this whole process to determine if it has been done thoroughly and accurately. Since it is often dealing with technical specialties in which only some (or none) of its members are trained, perfect certainty about the quality of the work may be unachievable. But by skillfully questioning the supporting analysis, the members of the regular meeting can usually assess the integrity of the recommendation.

2. If deficiencies are discovered in the recommendation, the regular meeting should not attempt to correct them unless they are very simple. The errors should simply be noted and taken into consideration in the final determination of how

to act on the recommendation—either to disapprove or redelegate. Regular meetings as a rule should not attempt to do task-force work.

3. The intense, critical examination that is typical of a good review may be intimidating for the presenter. To be best served by the presenter, the members should participate in a spirit of cooperative understanding. Once any of the participants in the meeting become defensive, the rational quality of the review usually diminishes.

REVIEWING RECOMMENDATIONS CHECK LIST

Examining the database:

Clarity

Readable formats

Sources understood

Time frames compatible

Definitions clear and consistent

Validity

Data-collection procedure

Bias free

Error free

All appropriate sources consulted

Constraints

Limits of data clear

Limits appropriate

Examining the interpretation of the data:

Alternatives considered

Assumptions of favored alternative

Problem definition, original thesis

Criteria used for evaluation

Priority of various criteria

Effects of history, tradition, policy

Positive and negative consequences of favored alternative

Comparative consequences of other alternatives

Assumed probabilities of consequences

Examining the conclusion or recommendation:

Conclusion in a nutshell

Changes required

Organizational mission or values

Policy

Structure

Leadership

Methods or procedures

Who is affected

How implemented

Schedule

Resources required

Who is accountable

RECOMMENDATIONS REVIEW
In a Nutshell

1. Presenter is introduced.
2. Presenter gives presentation:

   Expected response

   Preview of recommendation

   Brief description of process
3. Members question to assure accuracy and thoroughness (see check list).
4. Members advise leader whether or not to accept recommendation.
5. Leader summarizes and announces action to be taken.
6. Leader previews next steps and roles—commissioning.

➡ START/STOP/ALERT

When to Use This Procedure

1. When sharing news—especially if the members of your group typically bring several items that are strictly announcements requiring little or no deliberation;
2. When you want to encourage rapid and highly participative sharing of vital information among members of the group;
3. When you want a relevant but not too demanding warm-up of the participants early in the meeting.

Materials Needed

1. Note pad and pen or pencil for each member.

How to Use This Procedure

1. If this is the first time the group has used the procedure, the leader defines the terms:

   Start—What is new or proceeding in altered ways?

   Stop—What is completed or being discontinued?

   Alert—What problems or opportunities may be coming?
2. The leader gives each member of the group a turn to report starts.
3. The leader gives each member of the group a turn to report stops.
4. The leader gives each member of the group a turn to report alerts.
5. Leader summarizes.

Notes

1. It is a good idea to cover each agenda type in a separate round of sharing. This keeps the different moods pure. It also creates opportunity for everyone to participate more frequently.
2. It will sometimes be appropriate for the leader and other members to intervene to congratulate, commiserate, or accentuate the items reported.

START/STOP/ALERT
In a Nutshell

1. Define terms:

   Start—What's new

   Stop—What's at an end

   Alert—What's on the horizon (good or bad)
2. Each member reports starts.
3. Each member reports stops.
4. Each member reports alerts.
5. Leader summarizes.

→ *HIGHLIGHTS/LOWLIGHTS*[17]

When to Use This Procedure

1. When sharing news—especially if the members of your group typically bring several items that are strictly announcements requiring little or no deliberation;
2. When you want to encourage rapid and highly participative sharing of vital information among members of the group;
3. When you want a relevant but not too demanding warm-up of the participants early in the meeting.

Materials Needed

1. Note pad and pen or pencil for each member.

How to Use This Procedure

1. If this is the first time the group has used the procedure, the leader defines the terms:

   Highlights—Significant good news, accomplishments worth notice.

   Lowlights—Significant bad news, problems or failures worth notice as a warning or as a learning opportunity.

2. The leader asks each member to take a turn sharing at least one highlight and one lowlight. The leader explains that no member should pass—each member should share one of each. (Before the sharing begins, a couple of minutes may be allowed for preparation.)

---

[17]This procedure is often used at Intel Corporation.

3. The leader briefly summarizes and thanks the members for participation.

Notes

1. The leader discourages passing, because if a member does not share both a highlight and a lowlight he or she cheats the other members by leaving them unequally exposed. Often this will cause the other members to be more guarded in their participation and rob the procedure of its potential vitality.
2. Some groups have fun with this procedure. Highlights are followed with ritual applause or cheers; lowlights are followed with ritual silence or mournful sounds (such as that of a low fog horn). Some groups offer a revolving award for the best highlight and the best lowlight.
3. A time limit can be set for each person's turn.

HIGHLIGHTS/LOWLIGHTS
In a Nutshell

1. Define terms:

   Highlights—Good news

   Lowlights—Bad news
2. Each member shares at least one highlight and one lowlight.
3. Leader summarizes.

➡ FYI POSTERS

When to Use This Procedure

1. When sharing news—especially if the members of your group typically bring several items that are strictly announcements requiring little or no deliberation;
2. When you want to encourage rapid and highly participative sharing of vital information among members of the group;
3. When you want a relevant, but not too demanding warm-up of the participants early in the meeting.

Materials Needed

1. Flip-chart paper (one sheet per group member).
2. Felt-tipped markers (one per group member).
3. Masking tape.

How to Use This Procedure

1. Each member of the group (prior to the meeting or all at once during a five-minute period) uses a separate piece of flip-chart paper to list the news and issues he or she thinks ought to be discussed. The members should attempt to write each of these statements as a headline—thirteen words or less. Each member puts his or her name at the top of the chart.
2. All charts are hung on the wall side by side.
3. Where items have been duplicated on more than one chart, the item is kept on the chart farthest to the left and eliminated from all the others.

4. Participants read all the charts and initial those items they want to hear more about. No one should initial any of the items on his or her own chart. (All the members can work at this simultaneously.)

5. Items with two or more initials are discussed until interested parties are satisfied. (Two initials indicate that at least two others besides the author of the chart are interested.)

6. The leader asks if other (infrequently initialed) items need elaboration. Perhaps the item was listed in such a way that the other members of the group did not recognize its importance. If so, sixty seconds of elaboration is permitted.

7. The leader allows three minutes for participants to mill about and clean up remaining items in one-on-one conversations. (This period of time is essentially a "Flea Market," and the leader may want to review that procedure.)

Notes

It is a good idea to keep the members on their feet in front of the wall where the posters have been hung. Done correctly, this is a highly active process. Encourage a lively pace.

FYI POSTERS
In a Nutshell

1. Each member prepares poster on a flip chart:
   • Name at top
   • List of informational announcements
2. Posters are hung on the wall side by side.
3. Duplicate items are kept on poster farthest to the left.
4. Members initial items on others' charts that they want to know more about.
5. Only items with two or more initials are discussed.
6. Leader checks to see if infrequently initialized items need further elaboration.
7. Leader allows three minutes of milling about to settle other items.

➡ *FOR THE GOOD OF THE ORDER*[18]

When to Use This Procedure

1. When sharing news—especially if the members of your group typically bring several items that are strictly announcements requiring little or no deliberation;
2. When you want to encourage rapid and highly participative sharing of vital information among members of the group;
3. When you want a relevant, but not too demanding warm-up of the participants early in the meeting;
4. When you want to emphasize the accomplishments of the group.

Materials Needed

1. A note pad and pen or pencil for each member.

How to Use This Procedure

1. If this is the first time the group has used the procedure, the leader defines:
   For the good of the order—Significant good news; accomplishments on behalf of the organization worth noticing.
2. The leader asks each member to take a turn sharing at least one accomplishment for the good of the order that has been performed in his or her area of responsibility. The leader explains that no member should pass—that each member should share at least one accomplishment.

---

[18]This procedure was observed at meetings in the cities of Santee and Chula Vista in California.

3. The leader briefly summarizes and thanks the members for participation.

Notes

1. The leader should discourage passing, because if any one member does not share, it may make other members feel they have been immodest. Often this will cause the other members to be more guarded in their participation and rob the procedure of its potential vitality.
2. Some groups have fun with this procedure. Each report is followed with ritual applause or cheers. Some groups offer a revolving award for the best report.
3. A time limit can be set for each person's turn.

FOR THE GOOD OF THE ORDER
In a Nutshell

1. Leader defines *good of the order*—accomplishments on behalf of the organization worth noticing.
2. Each member shares at least one recent accomplishment.
3. Leader summarizes.

→ PROBLEM DEFINITION[19]

When to Use This Procedure

1. When group members seem to be trying to identify an issue that is so complex they cannot get hold of it.
2. When trying to clarify an issue in preparation for delegating it to one member or to a task force.
3. When a suggested issue seems important, but the way it has been stated does not help start the group discussion.

Materials Needed

1. Flip chart.
2. Felt-tipped markers.

How to Use This Procedure

Option A:

1. The leader asks the group to restate the problem in two sentences:

   Sentence 1: Describe the current, undesirable situation.

   Sentence 2: Describe the situation you want instead.

   > EXAMPLE: Given our current schedule, we will bring our new product to market four months later than our competitor. We need to beat our competitor to the market by at least sixty days.

---

[19]These problem definition options are adapted from procedures taught by the Saltwater Institute in Santa Cruz, California. Several other procedures are suggested in chapter 16 of *How to Make Meetings Work* (see footnote 7).

2. The leader asks the task force to which the group delegates the task (or in simple cases, the group itself) to list the steps that could be taken to get from the current situation to the desirable one.

Option B:

1. The leader asks the group members to restate the problem in a way that enables them to brainstorm the consequences of the problem.

    EXAMPLE: When our competitor brings its new product to market four months ahead of us the consequences for us will be. . .

2. The group brainstorms the list of consequences.
3. The group makes action plans for dealing with the important consequences.

Option C:

1. The leader asks the group to restate the problem in a way that enables it to brainstorm the causes.

    EXAMPLE: We are delayed in bringing our new product to market because. . .

2. The group brainstorms the list of causes.
3. The leader asks the task force to which the group delegates the task (or in simple cases, the group itself) to make action plans for dealing with the important causes.

PROBLEM DEFINITION
In a Nutshell

Option A:

1. State problem in two sentences:
    a. Describe current, undesirable situation.
    b. Describe desirable situation.
    (The difference between these two is the *problem.*)
2. List steps for getting from current to desirable situation. (Group may delegate this step.)

Option B:

1. Restate problem so group can brainstorm its consequences.
2. Brainstorm the consequences.
3. Make action plans for dealing with important consequences. (Group may delegate this step.)

Option C:

1. Restate problem so group can brainstorm its causes.
2. Brainstorm the causes.
3. Make action plans for dealing with important causes. (Group may delegate this step.)

➡ ASSIGNMENT MATRIX[20]

When to Use This Procedure

1. When you are summarizing the discussion of any item that will require further work;
2. When you are summarizing an entire meeting.

Materials Needed

1. Flip chart and felt-tipped markers or a prepared form.

How to Use This Procedure

1. Prior to the meeting, the leader prepares a flip chart or a form on which the following matrix has been constructed:

Follow-Up Items	Method	Deadline	LS	JV	DE	NM	CF	WD

The letters over the columns to the right of the "Deadline" column are the initials of the members of the meeting (a group of six people in this case).

---

[20]This procedure was observed at Intel Corporation.

2. As the meeting identifies items that need follow-up, the item is named in the first column. In the "Method" column, the group indicates if it is assigning the task ("A") or establishing a task force ("TF"). The deadline for the follow-up is indicated in the next column. An "X" can be placed in the column under the initials of the person(s) responsible.

3. After the meeting, a copy of the assignment matrix can be sent to each member of the group (with his or her column circled or highlighted) as a reminder of follow-up responsibilities.

Notes

Although a prepared form on regular notepaper may be used, also posting the assignment matrix on flip-chart paper helps the group keep track of its decisions and be mindful of how much work it is generating.

ASSIGNMENT MATRIX
In a Nutshell

1. Before meeting, prepare matrix with the following headings:

   Follow-Up Items   Method   Deadline   [Initials]

2. As follow-up items come up in meeting, record the acts of delegation in the matrix.

3. After meeting, send copies of matrix as a reminder.

➡ *FLEA MARKET*[21]

When to Use This Procedure

1. When you want to provide some time for the group members to resolve one-on-one business they have among themselves (see Note 1 below);
2. When you sense that time is being wasted on agenda items that really concern only two of the group's members and that the other members could use the same time profitably working with other unoccupied members of the group.

Materials Needed

1. Group members provide their own. (To facilitate this, the leader can show the period of time being set aside for "Flea Market" in the prepublished agenda.)

How to Use This Procedure

1. The leader explains to the group the ground rules for the Flea Market:
   - This time is to be used primarily for one-on-one business, though occasionally a subgroup of three or more may form. Avoid discussing agenda items that should involve the whole group.

---

[21]This procedure is adapted from the practice of Andrew Grove, the president and CEO of Intel Corporation.

- The agenda should be something that can be dealt with briefly—such as calendar coordination or checking on the status of an expected report.
- All members are to stay in the meeting room and remain available to each other for business. If they must remove themselves for purposes of confidentiality, they should return to the room as quickly as possible.
- Socializing is permissible, but those having business to do can interrupt social activity and take other members aside.

2. All members of the group stand up and move around the room to meet with those they need to talk to. If another member is already engaged, the waiting member works with someone else or stands by until the other is available.

3. Members who do not know of any business appropriate to conduct at this time remain in the room in case others want them. They may spend the time socially with other unoccupied members of the group but should be alert to others seeking their attention for business.

4. When the time set aside for the flea market has expired, the leader reconvenes the meeting for other work, or if the meeting is at an end, formally announces adjournment.

Notes

1. This procedure is especially helpful when the members of the meeting come from distances that keep them from being able to see one another on a daily basis. If they know that time will be set aside for a flea market, they can save up small issues that would otherwise take a lot of time to handle by telephone, memoranda, or electronic mail.

2. Refreshments may be made available during flea markets. This contributes to the informal, cocktail atmosphere appropriate to the procedure. Be careful, however, that the members understand that this is not just a time for socializing and that those who have one-on-one business to conduct with them have priority.

FLEA MARKET
In a Nutshell

1. Leader explains ground rules:

   Time for one-on-one business.

   Brief agendas.

   All members to remain in room.

   Business given priority over socializing.

   Time frame for flea market.

2. Members stand up and seek out those with whom they need to do one-on-one business.

3. Members without business initiate socialization unless interrupted for business.

4. Leader terminates flea market, reconvenes meeting, or announces formal adjournment.

➡ + / – *MEETING EVALUATION*[22]

When to Use This Procedure

1. When you want to increase the group's awareness of meeting procedures and engage their thinking on how to make meetings work better;
2. When you want to test the group's reactions to new procedures.

Materials Needed

1. Flip chart.
2. Felt-tipped markers.

How to Use This Procedure

1. At the end of the meeting, the leader takes a fresh flip-chart page and divides it into two columns with a vertical line drawn down the middle of the page. The left column is labeled with a plus ("+") and the right column with a minus ("–").
2. The leader asks the group to evaluate the meeting by answering the following questions:

   What worked well? (Chart answers under "+")

   What should we do more of?

   What did not work so well? (Chart answers under "–")

   What should be changed?

   What should be dropped?

---

[22]This procedure was observed at Intel Corporation.

3. The leader continues charting until the group slows down.
4. The leader uses this feedback in planning future meetings.

Notes

This should be a very quick procedure, with participants contributing concise comments, both positive and critical. It is especially useful after meetings in which new procedures have been tried.

+/− MEETING EVALUATION
In a Nutshell

1. At end of meeting, prepare flip chart:

    +   −

2. Evaluate meeting making two lists:

    On the plus side: On the minus side:
    What worked.   What didn't work.

3. Keep charting until group slows down.
4. Use feedback in planning future meetings.

Part 3:
Activities

1: SCREENING THE AGENDA FOR REGULAR MEETINGS

Objective

To identify the kinds of issues that are appropriate for regular meetings.

Process Objectives

1. To reinforce the distinction between *task-force* work and *regular-meeting* work.
2. To emphasize the four kinds of information appropriate for processing in regular meetings:
   - Pass Downs
   - Operational Reports
   - Task-Force Recommendations
   - News

Directions

1. Participants should review the sections in Part 1 headed "Identify Appropriate Kinds of Agenda" and "Screen the Agenda Before the Regular Meeting." Each participant works alone to sort the Items List into the Answer Grid, as instructed on the Directions sheet. (Ten minutes.)
2. The leader arranges the participants in subgroups of two to four members. These groups rework the problem to arrive at a subgroup answer using the Subgroup Performance Report. (Fifteen minutes.)

3. The leader provides a copy of the correct answers (see Appendix), so the subgroups may evaluate their work. (Three minutes.)

4. The leader conducts a discussion to deal with remaining questions. (Ten minutes.)

SCREENING THE AGENDA
FOR REGULAR MEETINGS
Directions

You are preparing the agenda for the next monthly regional sales meeting, typically an eight-hour session. Twelve district managers who report to you will be the participants. Suggested agenda items are listed with their presenters and time estimates on the next page.

All time estimates are conservative and assume (sometimes inappropriately) that the regular meeting will try to deal with the issue itself rather than delegate it to staff or a task force. If the regular meeting were to delegate these issues, the time could be cut to one-fourth of the current estimates.

Your task is to sort each item according to its agenda type and then determine if it should be on the agenda for this meeting.

- To show the agenda type, put an "X" in the appropriate column of the Answer Grid as demonstrated with the sample item.

- To show whether or not the item is to be included in this meeting's agenda, put a "Y" in the "Yes" column or an "N" in the "No" column.

- If an item should come on the agenda only to get the issue defined for delegation, mark the "Yes" column "Y-D" as demonstrated with the sample item.

- Other items may have to be put off for lack of time.

- Some of the items should not be on a regular-meeting agenda.

For assistance, review the sections on identifying and screening agenda in Part 1 of *Group Power II.*

SCREENING THE AGENDA FOR REGULAR MEETINGS
Items List

Sample: District 7 has discovered an outlet for the region's returned merchandise. We need a process to transfer, sell, and account for such merchandise. **Presenter:** District 7 Manager; two hours. (The Answer Grid shows how to categorize this sample.)

1. We need to review the sales figures from last month. **Presenters:** Managers; one hour.

2. You need to remind people about the quarterly-report deadline. **Presenter:** You; three minutes.

3. In response to your group's inquiries, engineering is prepared to present alternative color specifications for Product X. **Presenter:** Engineer; fifteen minutes.

4. Marketing wants a response to their recommendation on a possible new display shelf. **Presenter:** Marketing Director; thirty minutes.

5. You want to find out why Max, a salesperson in District 4, has such dramatically low sales figures this month. **Presenter:** You; ten minutes.

6. There is a new policy from headquarters concerning the schedule for paying commissions. **Presenter:** You; twenty minutes.

7. The region's training task force wants approval of a program to train the sales force how to introduce Product Q. This new product is to be brought to the market exactly five weeks after this regional meeting. The managers will be the trainers, so they must review the program to see if it meets objectives and to learn their trainer roles. **Presenter:** Trainer; three hours.

8. The Personnel Status Report shows unusually high turnover in our region—we want identification of causes and correction. **Presenter:** Personnel; two hours.

9. District 9 wants to announce that Alice, one of their salespeople, is the first in the region this year to pass the million-dollar mark in sales! **Presenter:** Manager; two minutes.

10. Sales records show we are below the goal for Product Z. We have to identify the cause and take corrective action. **Presenter:** You; two hours.

SCREENING THE AGENDA
FOR REGULAR MEETINGS
Answer Grid

Items	Agenda Type				Included?	
	Pass Down	Operations Report	Recommen- dation	News	Yes	No
Sample:				X __	Y-D	_____
1.					_____	_____
2.					_____	_____
3.					_____	_____
4.					_____	_____
5.					_____	_____
6.					_____	_____
7.					_____	_____
8.					_____	_____
9.					_____	_____
10.					_____	_____

SCREENING THE AGENDA
FOR REGULAR MEETINGS
Subgroup Performance Report

Directions:

1. On the table on the next page, list the member's individual choices first. After discussion, complete the Subgroup column.
2. After the leader gives you the answers, circle the incorrect items in the Subgroup column and discuss what led your group to misunderstand these items. Decide how you would avoid the same kind of error in the future.

Abbreviations:

Agenda Types: Included:
   P = Pass Down   Y = Yes
   O = Operations Review Y-D = Yes but Delegate
   R = Recommendations   N = No
   N = News

For each item, show the agenda type first, then whether it was included.

Items	Member 1	Member 2	Member 3	Member 4	Subgroup
0. Sample	N, Y-D	N, Y-D	N, Y-D	N, Y-D	N, Y-D
1. Sales report	_____	_____	_____	_____	_____
2. Quarterlies	_____	_____	_____	_____	_____
3. Color specs	_____	_____	_____	_____	_____
4. New shelf	_____	_____	_____	_____	_____
5. Max's sales	_____	_____	_____	_____	_____
6. Pay policy	_____	_____	_____	_____	_____
7. Training	_____	_____	_____	_____	_____
8. Turnover	_____	_____	_____	_____	_____
9. Alice	_____	_____	_____	_____	_____
10. Product Z	_____	_____	_____	_____	_____

⇨ 2: STRUCTURING MEMBERSHIP OF REGULAR MEETINGS

Objective

To determine the appropriate membership for a regular meeting given the organizational functions of the candidates.

Process Objectives

1. To reinforce the principles for determining membership for regular meetings.
2. To emphasize that the permanent membership of regular meetings mirrors the formal structure of the organization.

Directions

1. Participants should review "Structuring the Permanent Membership" in Part 1. Participants work alone to make a recommendation for how to structure the membership for The City Manager's Regular Meeting described on the Information Sheet. (Ten minutes.)
2. The leader arranges the participants in subgroups of two to four members. These groups rework the problem to arrive at a subgroup answer using the Subgroup Performance Report. (Fifteen minutes.)
3. The leader provides a copy of the correct answers (see Appendix), so the groups may evaluate their work. (Three minutes.)
4. The leader conducts a discussion to deal with remaining questions. (Ten minutes.)

STRUCTURING MEMBERSHIP OF REGULAR MEETINGS
Information Sheet

Directions: Read the background information about each of the candidates for permanent membership in the City Manager's regular meeting. Determine whether each candidate ought to be included or excluded. Be prepared to give a short rationale for your decisions. Record your answers on the Work Sheet.

The City Manager's Regular Meeting

This is the City Manager's highest level management meeting. At this meeting, held each Tuesday for ninety minutes, the City Manager wants to coordinate the operations of the city and assure that they are in accord with the City Council's policies. Since the City Council meets every other Monday, half of the City Manager's regular meetings deal with issues determined in the latest council meeting and with preparation for the next council meeting.

Candidates for Permanent Membership

Anderson. Chief of Police; reports directly to City Manager; large department.

Blackwell. Fire Chief; reports directly to City Manager; large department.

Carlton. Director of Public Works; reports directly to City Manager, large department.

Doolittle. Director of Parks & Recreation; reports directly to City Manager; large department.

Englehard. Director of Planning; reports directly to City Manager; small department.

Finnagan. Director of Central Services; reports directly to City Manager; small department.

Garcia. Director of Redevelopment; reports to Director of Planning; small department but high political profile.

Huskisson. Director of Transportation; reports to Director of Public Works; small department but has a major construction project underway that has a highly political profile and when completed next year will make the department large.

Ishmaelo. Assistant City Manager; reports directly to City Manager; is a staff assistant with special project responsibilities that sometimes give him direct authority over department heads and/or members of their departments.

Jackson. City Attorney; contracted by and reports directly to the Council; partner in his own law firm, very active in the operations of the City.

Klopper. City Clerk; elected official; functionally (though not formally) reporting to both the City Manager and the Council; manages the agenda and official records of the City Council; instrumental in linking the City's operations to Council Meetings.

Lovejoy. Director of Personnel; reports to Director of Central Services; frequently works directly and in confidence with both the City Manager and the City Council.

Morgan. Director of Finance; reports to Director of Central Services; crucial to the operations of the city and often a key management participant in Council Meetings.

Navarro. Director of Data Processing; reports to Director of Central Services; central to the computerized coordination of the City's operations and the answer man for many of the managers' most pressing questions.

Ostrander. Softball Coordinator; reports to Director of Parks and Recreation; largest program of citizen participation in the City.

Poletti. City Librarian; reports directly to City Manager; small department.

Querles. Director of Reference Services; reports to City Librarian; one-person function.

STRUCTURING MEMBERSHIP
OF REGULAR MEETINGS
Work Sheet

Members	Rationale	Excluded	Rationale
_____	_____	_____	_____
_____	_____	_____	_____
_____	_____	_____	_____
_____	_____	_____	_____
_____	_____	_____	_____
_____	_____	_____	_____
_____	_____	_____	_____
_____	_____	_____	_____
_____	_____	_____	_____
_____	_____	_____	_____
_____	_____	_____	_____
_____	_____	_____	_____
_____	_____	_____	_____
_____	_____	_____	_____
_____	_____	_____	_____
_____	_____	_____	_____
_____	_____	_____	_____

STRUCTURING MEMBERSHIP OF REGULAR MEETINGS
Subgroup Performance Report

Directions:

1. Use the abbreviations listed below in completing this form. List the member's individual choices first. After discussion, complete the Subgroup column.
2. After the leader gives you the answers, circle the incorrect items in the subgroup column and discuss what led your group to misunderstand these items. Decide how you would avoid the same kind of error in the future.

Abbreviations:

A = Anderson, Police
B = Blackwell, Fire
C = Carlton, Public Works
D = Doolittle, Parks & Rec.
E = Englehard, Planning
F = Finnagan, Central Services
G = Garcia, Redevelopment
H = Huskisson, Transportation
I = Ishmaelo, Assistant

J = Jackson, Attorney
K = Klopper, City Clerk
L = Lovejoy, Personnel
M = Morgan, Finance
N = Navarro, Data Processing
O = Ostrander, Softball
P = Poletti, Librarian
Q = Querles, Reference

Items	Member 1	Member 2	Member 3	Member 4	Subgroup
Members	_____	_____	_____	_____	_____
	_____	_____	_____	_____	_____
	_____	_____	_____	_____	_____
	_____	_____	_____	_____	_____
	_____	_____	_____	_____	_____

_____   _____   _____   _____   _____

_____   _____   _____   _____   _____

_____   _____   _____   _____   _____

_____   _____   _____   _____   _____

_____   _____   _____   _____   _____

_____   _____   _____   _____   _____

_____   _____   _____   _____   _____

_____   _____   _____   _____   _____

Excluded

_____   _____   _____   _____   _____

_____   _____   _____   _____   _____

_____   _____   _____   _____   _____

_____   _____   _____   _____   _____

_____   _____   _____   _____   _____

_____   _____   _____   _____   _____

_____   _____   _____   _____   _____

_____   _____   _____   _____   _____

_____   _____   _____   _____   _____

_____   _____   _____   _____   _____

_____   _____   _____   _____   _____

⇨ *3: RECOGNITION METHODS*

Objective

To generate as many ideas as possible about how to accomplish recognition at the beginning of regular meetings.

Process Objectives

1. To practice the brainstorming procedure.
2. To practice thinking in terms of symbolic behavior.

Directions

1. Participants should review the "Recognition" section in Part 1 (Five minutes.)
2. The leader arranges the participants in subgroups of three to seven members. Each subgroup selects a recorder from among its members. Each recorder is provided with a flip chart. (Two minutes.)
3. Participants read "Recognition Possibilities." (Three minutes.)
4. Subgroups *brainstorm* to generate as many ideas as possible about how to accomplish recognition at the beginning of regular meetings. The leader gives the following instructions:

   All ideas, however strange or impractical, should be recorded without evaluation. Try to keep the stream of ideas flowing continuously, keeping the recorders busy! Do not hesitate to "tailgate" on each other's ideas; that is, offer minor variations or elaborations. Think about the problem in the context of many different regular meetings; think about it with your eyes; think about it with your ears.

   (Ten minutes.)

5. After the brainstorm session, each recorder numbers the ideas on the flip chart. Subgroups select from their lists two or three ideas that would work well in at least one regular meeting. (Three minutes.)

6. A presenter from each subgroup (someone besides the recorder) shares the subgroup's ideas with the rest of the large group. (One minute per subgroup.)

RECOGNITION METHODS
Recognition Possibilities

Here are some ideas to stimulate thinking about ways to accomplish recognition at the beginning of regular meetings.

VISUAL

- Have guests, if any, assemble in the meeting room first. Have permanent members come in last from another assembly area with the meeting leader in the lead or bringing up the rear (i.e., in a processional).
- Seat only permanent members at the conference table, with the leader at the head, and seat all other participants in chairs surrounding the table at a short distance.
- For permanent members only, provide the agenda and other meeting documents in leather binders; for all other participants, provide the documents as unbound handouts.
- Mark the seats or table locations of the permanent members with placards or brass plates bearing their titles.
- Use special styles or colors of chairs to denote the various ranks of permanent members and guests.
- Use special styles or colors of name tags for the various ranks of permanent members and guests.
- Ask all permanent members to take off their jackets (and ties?); ask all guests to appear in coat and tie.
- During the first minutes of the meeting, have only the permanent members stand for some ritual (e.g., roll call, leader's reading, or statement about their responsibilities as permanent members).

AUDITORY

- Roll call, by name and title.
- Each permanent member takes a minute at the start of the meeting to share one highlight from his or her part of the organization, some performance noteworthy for its excellence.

- The leader begins the meeting by polling only the permanent members to see if any have guests to introduce or additions or corrections to the agenda.
- The leader begins the meeting by polling only the permanent members to assure that they and their guests have signed nondisclosure forms concerning the proceedings of the meeting.
- The leader begins the meeting on a light note by describing a picture (perhaps of some recent and humorous event in the life of the organization) and asking each permanent member to provide a caption for the picture.
- The leader begins the meeting on a light note by asking each permanent member to answer the question, "What is the title of one book on the top shelf of your bookcase?"

4. IDENTIFYING PARTICIPANT SKILLS

Objective

To match dialog with participant skills.

Process Objectives

1. To practice identifying the participant skills.
2. To prepare for observing participant skills in later activities.

Directions

1. Each participant works alone on the Work Sheet to match each of the eleven pieces of dialog with the participant skill it best illustrates. (Eight minutes.)
2. Participants are assigned to a subgroup of four to six members. Sharing the work they did while working alone, the subgroup members rework the activity to achieve consensus. (Ten minutes.)
3. The leader provides the correct answers (see Appendix).
4. The subgroups review and correct any errors.
5. The leader conducts a discussion to resolve any remaining questions. (Ten minutes.)

IDENTIFYING PARTICIPANT SKILLS
Work Sheet

Directions: Match each piece of dialog with the participant skill it best illustrates. Place the letter of the skill in the space in front of the dialog number. (Refer to the section on "Participant Skills" in Section 1 of *Group Power II.*)

Participant Skills

A = Initiating

B = Providing Info. and Opinion

C = Asking for Info. and Opinion

D = Clarifying

E = Elaborating

F = Summarizing

G = Compromising

H = Gatekeeping

I = Harmonizing

J = Testing the Norm State

K = Encouraging

Dialog

_____ 1. "I'm taking a lot of these questions more personally than I ought to. I'd appreciate a short break while I try to cool off a little."

_____ 2. "I'd like to shift the group's attention to the potentially negative consequences of the alternatives we are considering."

_____ 3. "If we go for the first alternative, the follow-on costs will be greater and will probably grow by 10 to 15 percent each year."

_____ 4. "It's frustrating not having an option that will be popular—which is all the more reason to make sure our conclusion reflects the kind of thorough analysis we've been doing so far and to keep on doing it."

_____ 5. "When Bob says the follow-on costs of the first alternative will be greater, he means there will be a greater need for software modifications."

_____ 6. "How do the follow-on costs of these alternatives compare?"

_____   7. "So far, we've only been evaluating the negative consequences of the first alternative, and only the follow-
on costs have been mentioned."

_____   8. "I think we can get both the faster hardware of the first
alternative and the more stable software of the second
alternative. I've heard they are operating compatibly at
our plant in Phoenix."

_____   9. "How should we interpret your silence on this,
Sarah?"

_____   10. "If we keep in mind the newness of this vendor, the
follow-on costs Bob has mentioned may be even
higher."

_____   11. "Wouldn't we work more efficiently if we broke into
subgroups rather than try to do all of this as one large
group?"

⇨ 5. PARTICIPANT SKILLS ASSESSMENT

Objectives

1. To identify which participant skills one uses most and least frequently.
2. To review the uses and misuses of these same participant skills.

Process Objectives

1. To increase understanding of participant skills.
2. To develop awareness of one's own tendencies in group participation.
3. To prepare for observing participant behavior in later activities.

Directions

1. Working alone, each participant reviews the Eleven Participant Skills and identifies the three skills he or she uses *most frequently* and the three he or she uses *least frequently.* (Five minutes.)
2. In subgroups of four or five members, the participants share with one another which of the participant skills they use most and least frequently. (Ten minutes.)
3. Remaining in their subgroups, but working alone, participants select from the list of participant skills:

a. The three skills that are most often abused (overused) by an individual to dominate the group. (Dominate is defined as "blocking or controlling the group's access to the resources by any of its members.")

b. The two skills that when used appropriately most easily allow a person to empower the participation of other group members.

Participants share their ideas in their subgroup, and the subgroup attempts to reach consensus on the answers. (Ten minutes.)

4. The leader shares the correct answers (see Appendix) to Step 3 with the class and asks the subgroups to review their work. (Three minutes.)

5. The leader conducts a discussion with the whole group to answer remaining questions. (Ten minutes.)

PARTICIPANT SKILLS ASSESSMENT
Eleven Participant Skills

Initiating. Someone gets the ball rolling both at the beginning and at critical transitions of the meeting.

Providing Information and Opinions. Everyone comes prepared to offer relevant information and has a sense of obligation to do so.

Asking for Information and Opinions. This is especially important for pointing out omissions in the data base.

Clarifying. Restating a point to make sure it is understood.

Elaborating. The ability to see the implications of an idea and add examples to emphasize a point.

Summarizing. Stating what has been accomplished so far in a way that also focuses on where the group is in its procedures and looks toward next steps.

Compromising. Finding a rational unity between conflicting ideas.

Gatekeeping. Inviting a silent member to speak or turning attention away from one who talks too much.

Harmonizing. The ability to calm others and relieve them of emotions that start getting in the way of good thinking.

Testing the Group's Norm State. Calling direct attention to behaviors that seem to distort the group's proper norm state. Be careful! First try this skill with the meeting leader in private.

Encouraging. Helping the group deal with frustration and low morale, sometimes by recalling past successes.

⇨ 6: OPERATIONS REVIEW MEETING 1

Objective

To review the performance of some of the subgroups on the activity "Screening the Agenda for Regular Meetings," which was done earlier in this training program.

Note: To do this activity, the group should first complete Activity 1, "Screening the Agenda for Regular Meetings."

Process Objectives

1. To be observed and coached by a partner in practicing participant skills.
2. To practice the following procedures:
   - Operations Review
   - +/− Meeting Evaluation

Directions

1. The trainer will be the leader for this meeting or will appoint someone else as leader. The leader prepares by reading the Leader's Instructions sheet. (Five minutes.)
2. The trainer arranges the participants in subgroups of two to four members each. These can be the same subgroups who worked together in the agenda-screening activity. Then one member from each subgroup is selected (or appointed by the trainer); these representatives sit in a semicircle facing a flip chart. The trainer chooses three of the representatives to be presenters and report on the performance of

their subgroups. (More than three presenters may be selected if time permits.) The representatives prepare by reading the Representative's Instructions sheet. (Five minutes.)

3. The other members of the subgroups will serve as observers of their own representative. Observers sit outside the semicircle where they can see the face of their own representative. They prepare by reading the Observer's Work Sheet. (Five minutes.)

4. The trainer or appointed leader conducts the staff meeting according to the following agenda. (Twenty minutes.)

AGENDA

Items	Procedure	Responsible
Activity Subgroup 1	Operations Review	All Participants
Activity Subgroup 2	Operations Review	All Participants
Activity Subgroup 3	Operations Review	All Participants

5. While the meeting is in progress, the observers chart their representative's performance in the meeting by using the Observer's Work Sheet.

6. After the meeting, the representatives meet briefly with their observers to discuss the notes made in all sections of the Observer's Work Sheet. (Three minutes.)

7. The observers change seats with the representatives, taking the inner ring, and evaluate the staff meeting by using the +/– Meeting Evaluation procedure. (Five minutes.)

OPERATIONS REVIEW MEETING 1
Leader's Instructions

If you have any questions after reading these instructions, call on your trainer for assistance before the meeting begins.

You will conduct this meeting by using the Operations Review Procedure as indicated on the following agenda:

AGENDA

Items	Procedure	Responsible
Activity Subgroup 1	Operations Review	All Participants
Activity Subgroup 2	Operations Review	All Participants
Activity Subgroup 3	Operations Review	All Participants

To conduct the meeting means to:
1. Guide the group members through the steps of the procedure.
2. Encourage their participation.

The participants will be offering information and ideas based on subgroup performance of the activity, "Screening the Agenda for Regular Meetings," completed earlier in this training program. At no time will they deliberately create distractions or difficulties, but if these occur, handle them as graciously as you can.

This meeting should last only twenty minutes, so encourage a lively pace of participation.

The following is your preparation check list:

1. Review the Operations Review procedure in the "Procedures" section (Part 2). The presenters will be reporting the performances recorded on the Subgroup Performance Report from the agenda-screening activity.
2. Prepare the following flip chart on which to summarize the subgroup reports:

SUBGROUP REPORTS

Performance Standard: 80%

Correct Answers		Subgroups		
		1	2	3
Sample	N, Y-D			
1. Sales	OR, Y			
2. Quarterlies	PD, Y			
3. Color	R, Y			
4. Shelf	R, Y			
5. Max	OR, N			
6. Pay	PD, Y			
7. Training	R, Y			
8. Turnover	OR, Y-D			
9. Alice	N, Y			
10. Z Sales	OR, Y-D			
Percentage Correct:	100%	_____	_____	_____

3. Ask the presenters to fill in their subgroup's column on the flip chart before beginning the meeting and to highlight in red their errors.

4. Begin the meeting by asking each presenter to briefly describe his or her subgroup's performance. If errors were made, ask what decisions were made to avoid such errors in the future. After these presentations have been made, encourage the group to identify any patterns in the success or failure of these subgroups, to evaluate the probable effectiveness of the corrective actions the subgroups decided on, and to suggest any other corrective actions that might be appropriate. Summarize the discussion, being sure to make the following points:

   What corrective actions taken by the subgroups are acceptable.

   What other corrective actions, if any, are necessary.

   What parts of the subgroups' performances were exemplary.

OPERATIONS REVIEW MEETING 1
Representative's Instructions

The meeting will be conducted by using the Operations Review Procedure as indicated on the following agenda:

AGENDA

Items	Procedure	Responsible
Activity Subgroup 1	Operations Review	All Participants
Activity Subgroup 2	Operations Review	All Participants
Activity Subgroup 3	Operations Review	All Participants

The leader will guide the group through the procedure.

You are to offer counsel to the leader in evaluating the performance of some subgroups on the activity "Screening the Agenda for Regular Meetings," which was completed earlier in this training program. The purpose of the discussion is to commend good performance and assure that sufficient corrective action has been taken where necessary.

The following is your preparation check list:

1. Review the Operations Review procedure in the "Procedures" section (Part 2). Your leader will use the procedure to conduct this meeting.
2. Review the activity "Screening the Agenda for Regular Meetings" and the answer sheet in the Appendix. Performance of the subgroups on this activity will be the subject of the review.
3. Review Section A of the Observer's Work Sheet. Notice the different kinds of participation that your observer will be watching for and look for opportunities during the meeting to exhibit these skills.
4. *If you have been appointed as a presenter in this meeting:*
   - Review your subgroup's performance on the Subgroup Performance Report from the agenda-screening activity. Before the meeting begins, record your subgroup's answers, highlighting the errors in red, on the flip chart prepared by the leader of the meeting.

- Be prepared to make the presentation required in Step 1 of the Operations Review procedure from the "Procedures" section (Part 2).
- Give special attention to the presentation outline suggested by Section B of the Observer's Work Sheet.

The primary purpose of this activity is to become familiar with the procedures. Cooperate with the leader to help the group through the activity. *Do not in any deliberate way create distractions or difficulties for the group or the leader.*

The group must get through this meeting in twenty minutes. This means you must participate at a lively pace.

If you have any questions after reading these instructions, call on your trainer for assistance before the meeting begins.

OPERATIONS REVIEW MEETING 1
Observer's Work Sheet

SECTION A

Directions: Each time your representative speaks, make a tally mark in the chart below to show which kind of participation the comment is. (For definitions see "Participant Skills" in Part 1 under the "Participating in Regular Meetings" section.)

Task Skills

(used by my representative)
>   Initiating
>   Providing information/opinion
>   Asking for information
>   Clarifying
>   Elaborating
>   Summarizing
>   Compromising

Maintenance Skills

(used by my representative)
>   Gatekeeping
>   Harmonizing
>   Testing norm states
>   Encouraging

Other Observations

1. Was my representative's nonverbal participation constructive?
2. Did my representative appear to pay attention to the others as they spoke?
3. Was my representative helpful to the leader?
4. Did my representative act responsibly for the smooth operation of the meeting?

SECTION B

Directions: If your representative is a presenter in this meeting, observe the presentation with this check list:

_____ Opened with a statement of response expected from group (e.g., "I expect your approval" or "I need your help on a problem").

_____ Briefly described performance vs. standard.

_____ Reported corrective actions taken.

_____ Reported causes for excellence.

SECTION C

Directions: Before the meeting, review the procedures (in Part 2) that will be used:

Operations Review
+ / – Meeting Evaluation

As the meeting proceeds, pay attention to how the procedures are used. When the meeting is over, you will trade places with your representative. With the other observers, you will evaluate the staff meeting by using the + / – Meeting Evaluation procedure.

⇨ 7: OPERATIONS REVIEW MEETING 2

Objective

To review the performance of some of the subgroups on the activity "Structuring Membership of Regular Meetings," which was done earlier in this training program.

Note: To do this activity, the group should first complete the activity "Structuring Membership of Regular Meetings."

Process Objectives

1. To be observed and coached by a partner in practicing participant skills.
2. To practice these two procedures:
   - Operations Review
   - +/– Meeting Evaluation

Directions

1. The trainer will be the leader for this meeting or will appoint someone else as leader. The leader prepares by reading the Leader's Instructions sheet. (Five minutes.)
2. The trainer arranges the participants in subgroups of two to four members each. These can be the same subgroups who worked together in the agenda-screening activity. Then one member from each subgroup is selected (or appointed by the trainer); these representatives sit in a semicircle facing a flip chart. The trainer chooses three of the representatives to be presenters and report on the performance of

their subgroups. (More than three presenters may be selected if time permits.) The representatives prepare by reading the Representative's Instructions sheet. (Five minutes.)

3. The other members of the subgroups will serve as observers of their own representative. Observers sit outside the semicircle where they can see the face of their own representative. They prepare by reading the Observer's Work Sheet. (Five minutes.)

4. The trainer or appointed leader conducts the staff meeting according to the following agenda. (Twenty minutes.)

AGENDA

Items	Procedure	Responsible
Activity Subgroup 1	Operations Review	All Participants
Activity Subgroup 2	Operations Review	All Participants
Activity Subgroup 3	Operations Review	All Participants

5. While the meeting is in progress, the observers chart their representative's performance in the meeting by using the Observer's Work Sheet.

6. After the meeting, the representatives meet briefly with their observers to discuss the notes made in all sections of the Observer's Work Sheet. (Three minutes.)

7. The observers change seats with the representatives, taking the inner ring, and evaluate the staff meeting by using the + / − Meeting Evaluation procedure. (Five minutes.)

OPERATIONS REVIEW MEETING 2
Leader's Instructions

You will conduct this meeting by using the Operations Review Procedure as indicated on the following agenda:

AGENDA

Items	Procedure	Responsible
Activity Subgroup 1	Operations Review	All Participants
Activity Subgroup 2	Operations Review	All Participants
Activity Subgroup 3	Operations Review	All Participants

To conduct the meeting means to:

1. Guide the group members through the steps of the procedure.
2. Encourage their participation.

The participants will be offering information and ideas based on subgroup performance of the activity "Structuring Membership of Regular Meetings," completed earlier in this training program. At no time will they deliberately create distractions or difficulties, but if these occur, handle them as graciously as you can.

This meeting should last only twenty minutes, so encourage a lively pace of participation.

The following is your preparation check list:

1. Review the Operations Review procedure in the "Procedures" section (Part 2). The presenters will be reporting the performances recorded on the Subgroup Performance Report from the activity "Structuring Membership of Regular Meetings."
2. Prepare flip chart (see "Subgroup Reports" on next page) on which to summarize the subgroup reports:
3. Ask the presenters to fill in their subgroup's column on the flip chart before beginning the meeting and to highlight in red their errors.

SUBGROUP REPORTS

Performance Standard: 77% (14 of 17 correct)

	Subgroups		
Correct Answers	1	2	3
Members			
1. Anderson			
2. Blackwell			
3. Carlton			
4. Doolittle			
5. Englehard			
6. Finnagan			
7. Poletti			
Excluded			
8. Garcia			
9. Huskisson			
10. Ishmaelo			
11. Jackson			
12. Klopper			
13. Lovejoy			
14. Morgan			
15. Navarro			
16. Ostrander			
17. Querles			
Number Correct: 17	_____	_____	_____

4. Begin the meeting by asking each presenter to briefly describe his or her subgroup's performance. If errors were made, ask what decisions were made to avoid such errors in the future. After these presentations have been made, encourage the group to identify any patterns in the success or failure of these subgroups, to evaluate the probable effectiveness of the corrective actions the subgroups decided on, and to suggest any other corrective actions that might be appropriate. Summarize the discussion, being sure to make the following points:

What corrective actions taken by the subgroups are acceptable.

What other corrective actions, if any, are necessary.

What parts of the subgroups' performances were exemplary.

If you have any questions after reading these instructions, call on your trainer for assistance before the meeting begins.

OPERATIONS REVIEW MEETING 2
Representative's Instructions

The meeting will be conducted by using the Operations Review Procedure as indicated on the following agenda:

AGENDA

Items	Procedure	Responsible
Activity Subgroup 1	Operations Review	All Participants
Activity Subgroup 2	Operations Review	All Participants
Activity Subgroup 3	Operations Review	All Participants

The leader will guide the group through the procedure.

You are to offer counsel to the leader in evaluating the performance of some subgroups on the activity "Structuring Membership of Regular Meetings," which was completed earlier in this training program. The purpose of the discussion is to commend good performance and assure that sufficient corrective action has been taken where necessary.

The following is your preparation check list:

1. Review the Operations Review procedure in the "Procedures" section (Part 2). Your leader will use the procedure to conduct this meeting.

2. Review the activity "Structuring Membership of Regular Meetings" and the answer sheet in the Appendix. Performance of the subgroups on this activity will be the subject of the review.

3. Review Section A of the Observer's Work Sheet. Notice the different kinds of participation that your observer will be watching for and look for opportunities during the meeting to exhibit these skills.

4. *If you have been appointed as a presenter in this meeting:*

   • Review your subgroup's performance on the Subgroup Performance Report from the structuring-membership activity. Before the meeting begins, record your subgroup's answers, highlighting the errors in red, on the flip chart prepared by the leader of the meeting.

- Be prepared to make the presentation required in Step 1 of the Operations Review procedure from the "Procedures" section (Part 2).
- Give special attention to the presentation outline suggested by Section B of the Observer's Work Sheet.

The primary purpose of this activity is to become familiar with the procedures. Cooperate with the leader to help the group through the activity. *Do not in any deliberate way create distractions or difficulties for the group or the leader.*

The group must get through this meeting in twenty minutes. This means you must participate at a lively pace.

If you have any questions after reading these instructions, call on your trainer for assistance before the meeting begins.

OPERATIONS REVIEW MEETING 2
Observer's Work Sheet

SECTION A

Directions: Each time your representative speaks, make a tally mark in the chart below to show which kind of participation the comment is. (For definitions see "Participant Skills" in Part 1 under the "Participating in Regular Meetings" section.)

Task Skills
(used by my representative)

Initiating

Providing information/opinion

Asking for information

Clarifying

Elaborating

Summarizing

Compromising

Maintenance Skills
(used by my representative)

Gatekeeping

Harmonizing

Testing norm states

Encouraging

Other Observations

1. Was my representative's nonverbal participation constructive?

2. Did my representative appear to pay attention to the others as they spoke?

3. Was my representative helpful to the leader?

4. Did my representative act responsibly for the smooth operation of the meeting?

Additional Observations:

SECTION B

Directions: If your representative is a presenter in this meeting, observe the presentation with this check list:

_____ Opened with a statement of response expected from group (e.g., "I expect your approval" or "I need your help on a problem").

_____ Briefly described performance vs. standard.

_____ Reported corrective actions taken.

_____ Reported causes for excellence.

SECTION C

Directions: Before the meeting, review the procedures (in Part 2) that will be used:

Operations Review
+ / − Meeting Evaluation

As the meeting proceeds, pay attention to how the procedures are used. When the meeting is over, you will trade places with your representative. With the other observers, you will evaluate the staff meeting by using the + / − Meeting Evaluation procedure.

⇨ 8: START UP STAFF MEETING 1

Objective

To begin a staff meeting by securing commitment to a pass down and by sharing news.

Process Objectives

1. To be observed and coached by a partner in practicing both task and maintenance skills.
2. To practice four different procedures for staff meetings:
   - Case Studies
   - Start/Stop/Alert
   - Assignment Matrix
   - +/− Meeting Evaluation

Directions

1. The trainer will be the leader for this meeting or will appoint someone else as leader. The leader prepares by following the Leader's Instructions sheet. (Five minutes.)
2. The trainer divides the group into two subgroups: participants and observers. Each observer is assigned to a particular participant. In the event of an odd number of members, one participant will be assigned two observers.
3. Participants sit in an inner circle; observers, in an outer circle. Observers position themselves so that they can see the faces of their partners. Participants prepare by reading the Participant's Instructions sheet; observers, by reading the Observer's Work Sheet. (Five minutes.)

4. The trainer or the assigned leader conducts the staff meeting according to the following agenda. (Twenty minutes.)

AGENDA

Items	Procedure	Responsible
Pass Downs	Case Studies	Group Leader
News	Stop/Start/Alert	All Participants
Summary	Assignment Matrix	All Participants

5. While the meeting is being conducted, the observers chart their partners' performance in the meeting by using the Observer's Work Sheet.

6. After the meeting, each participant meets briefly with his or her observing partner to discuss the notes made in both sections of the Observer's Work Sheet. (Five minutes.)

7. The observers change seats with the participants, taking the inner ring, and evaluate the staff meeting by using the + / – Meeting Evaluation procedure.

START UP STAFF MEETING 1
Leader's Instructions

Start this staff meeting by using the procedures indicated on the following agenda:

AGENDA

Items	Procedure	Responsible
Pass Downs	Case Studies	Group Leader
News	Stop/Start/Alert	All Participants
Summary	Assignment Matrix	All Participants

To conduct the meeting means to:

1. Guide the participants through the steps of the procedures.
2. Encourage their participation.

The participants will offer information and ideas based on their real-world roles at work. At no time will they deliberately create distractions or difficulties, but if these occur, handle them as graciously as you can.

This meeting should last about twenty minutes, so encourage a lively pace of participation. Remind your group of this time limit at the beginning of the meeting.

The following is your preparation check list:

1. Review the Assignment Matrix procedure in Part 2. Prepare an assignment matrix on a flip chart. Start your meeting by asking participants to "sign in" on the matrix. They should give the group their names, put their initials on the chart, and if appropriate, tell the group their organization and title. The matrix will be available to the group for use at any time during the meeting.
2. Review the Case Studies procedure in Part 2. Review the Pass Down Case Study, which follows these instructions.
3. Review the Start/Stop/Alert procedures in Part 2. Think about how you will introduce and summarize this part of the meeting. Be prepared to use the assignment matrix.
4. Stop the activity and thank the group for its participation. Remind everyone that this was only the start of a staff meeting and that the next procedures on the agenda would be Operations Review and Recommendations Review.

START UP STAFF MEETING 1
Pass Down Case Study

There is considerable evidence that regular meetings are being held without well-managed agendas. All managers in this organization are required to give this matter serious attention and to take corrective action (for your own meetings and for those of your subordinates). In three months, an audit will be conducted to assess compliance with this pass down.

To assure your understanding of well-managed agendas, consider the following case in which the manager makes a number of errors. Please read it and list the mistakes you notice. Review the recommendations in the "Controlling the Agenda" section in Part 1.

On Thursday mornings the staff gathers in the manager's conference room. (There is usually a delay while the manager's secretary calls around to find out why some members have not shown up and to find out when they will do so.) When the meeting begins, the manager hands out a list of the things he wants to cover in the meeting.

EXAMPLE:

Budget deadlines.
Holiday vacation schedule.
Why is report XYZ of Department 1 not in?
How to stop service complaints.
Report from representatives attending a regional conference.
Update on Sally's condition in the hospital.

Occasionally there will be other charts or reports handed out as back-up material for discussion of some of the items. During the meeting, the manager discourages members from bringing up anything not on his list. He expects everything else to be handled with him personally or among the members outside the meeting.

START UP STAFF MEETING 1
Participant's Instructions

The meeting will be started by using the procedures indicated on the following agenda. The leader will guide the group through these procedures.

AGENDA

Items	Procedure	Responsible
Pass Downs	Case Studies	Group Leader
News	Stop/Start/Alert	All Participants
Summary	Assignment Matrix	All Participants

Offer information and ideas based on your real-world role at work. Before the meeting, think about what you will say at each step in the procedures. Be prepared to ask questions or make comments about the issues raised by others. The primary purpose of the activity is to become familiar with the procedures. Cooperate with your leader to help the group through the activity. *Do not in any deliberate way create distractions or difficulties for the group or the leader.*

The meeting will last twenty minutes. This means you must participate at a lively pace.

The following is your preparation check list:

1. Review the Case Studies procedure in Part 2. Your leader will use this procedure in communicating the pass down.
2. Review the Start/Stop/Alert procedure in Part 2. Think about what you will say when called on in this part of the meeting.
3. Review the Assignment Matrix procedure in Part 2. Your leader will use this procedure as appropriate throughout the start of this meeting.
4. Review Section A of the Observer's Work Sheet. Notice the different kinds of participation that your partner will be watching for and look for opportunities during the meeting to exhibit these skills.

START UP STAFF MEETING 1
Observer's Work Sheet

SECTION A

Directions: Each time your partner speaks, make a tally mark in the chart below to show which kind of participation the comment is. (For definitions see "Participant Skills" in Part 1 under the "Participating in Regular Meetings" section.)

Task Skills
(used by my partner)
> Initiating
> Providing information/opinion
> Asking for information
> Clarifying
> Elaborating
> Summarizing
> Compromising

Maintenance Skills
(used by my partner)
> Gatekeeping
> Harmonizing
> Testing norm states
> Encouraging

Other Observations

1. Was my partner's nonverbal participation constructive?
2. Did my partner appear to pay attention to the others as they spoke?
3. Was my partner helpful to the leader?
4. Did my partner act responsibly for the smooth operation of the meeting?

Additional Observations:

SECTION B

Directions: Before the meeting, review the procedures in Part 2 that will be used:

Case Studies
Start/Stop/Alert
Assignment Matrix
+/− Meeting Evaluation

As the meeting proceeds, pay attention to how the procedures are used. When the meeting is over, you will trade places with your partner. With the other observers, you will evaluate the staff meeting by using the +/− Meeting Evaluation procedure.

⇨ *9: START UP STAFF MEETING 2*

Objective

To begin a staff meeting by sharing news and building an agenda.

Process Objectives

1. To be observed and coached by a partner in practicing both task and maintenance skills;
2. To practice five different procedures for staff meetings:
   - FYI Posters
   - Agenda Building
   - Expected Response
   - Assignment Matrix
   - +/− Meeting Evaluation

Directions

1. The trainer will be the leader for this meeting or will appoint someone else as leader. The leader prepares by reading the Leader's Instructions sheet. (Five minutes.)
2. The trainer divides the group into two subgroups: participants and observers. Each observer is assigned to a particular participant. In the event of an odd number of members, one participant will be assigned two observers.
3. Participants sit in an inner circle; observers, in an outer circle. Observers position themselves so that they can see the faces of their partners. Participants prepare by reading the Participant's Instructions sheet; observers, by reading the Observer's Work Sheet. (Five minutes.)

4. The trainer or the assigned leader conducts the staff meeting according to the following agenda. (Twenty minutes.)

AGENDA

Items	Procedure	Responsible
News	FYI Posters	Group Leader
Open Items	Agenda Building	All Participants
	Expected Response	All Participants
Summary	Assignment Matrix	All Participants

5. While the meeting is being conducted, the observers chart their partners' performance in the meeting by using the Observer's Work Sheet.

6. After the meeting, each participant meets briefly with his or her observing partner to discuss the notes made in both sections of the Observer's Work Sheet. (Five minutes.)

7. The observers change seats with the participants, taking the inner ring, and evaluate the staff meeting by using the +/− Meeting Evaluation procedure.

START UP STAFF MEETING 2
Leader's Instructions

Start this staff meeting by using the procedures indicated on the following agenda:

AGENDA

Items	Procedure	Responsible
News	FYI Posters	Group Leader
Open Items	Agenda Building	All Participants
	Expected Response	All Participants
Summary	Assignment Matrix	All Participants

To conduct the meeting means to:

1. Guide the group members through the steps of the procedures.
2. Encourage their participation.

The participants will offer information and ideas based on their real-world roles at work. At no time will they deliberately create distractions or difficulties, but if these occur, handle them as graciously as you can.

This meeting should last about twenty minutes, so encourage a lively pace of participation. Remind your group of this time limit at the beginning of the meeting.

The following is your preparation check list:

1. Review the Assignment Matrix procedure in Part 2. Prepare an assignment matrix on a flip chart. Start your meeting by asking participants to "sign in" on the matrix. They should give the group their names, put their initials on the chart, and if appropriate, tell the group their organization and title. The matrix will be available to the group for use at any time during the meeting.
2. Review the FYI Posters procedure in Part 2. Think about how you will introduce and summarize this part of the meeting. Be prepared to use the assignment matrix.

3. Review the Agenda Building and the Expected Response procedures in Part 2. You can combine these two procedures by asking each participant who suggests an issue for discussion to name the expected response. Make a note on the flip chart to indicate the expected response.

Note: After the group has spent a little time discussing some of these items, your trainer may interrupt to shorten the meeting.

4. Stop the activity and thank the group for its participation. Remind everyone that this was only the start of a staff meeting and that probably the next procedures on the agenda would be Operations Review and Recommendations Review.

If you have any questions after reading these instructions, call on your trainer for assistance before the meeting begins.

START UP STAFF MEETING 2
Participant's Instructions

The meeting will be started by using the procedures indicated on the following agenda. The leader will guide the group through these procedures.

AGENDA

Items	Procedure	Responsible
News	FYI Posters	Group Leader
Open Items	Agenda Building	All Participants
	Expected Response	All Participants
Summary	Assignment Matrix	All Participants

Offer information and ideas based on your real-world role at work. Before the meeting, think about what you will say at each step in the procedures. Be prepared to ask questions or make comments about the issues raised by others. The primary purpose of the activity is to become familiar with the procedures. Cooperate with your leader to help the group through the activity. *Do not in any deliberate way create distractions or difficulties for the group or the leader.*

The meeting will last twenty minutes. This means you must participate at a lively pace.

The following is your preparation check list:

1. Review the FYI Posters procedure in Part 2. Prepare your poster on flip-chart paper before the meeting begins.
2. Review the Agenda Building and the Expected Response procedures in Part 2. Think of at least one issue that you think participants in this group would find interesting to discuss. Be prepared to discuss this topic during the agenda building and also be prepared to indicate the expected response.

   Note: After the group has spent a little time discussing some of these items, your trainer may interrupt to shorten the meeting.

3. Review the Assignment Matrix procedure in Part 2. Your leader will use this procedure to summarize your meeting.

4. Review Section A of the Observer's Work Sheet. Notice the different kinds of participation that your partner will be watching for and look for opportunities during the meeting to exhibit these skills.

If you have any questions after reading these instructions, call on your trainer for assistance before the meeting begins.

START UP STAFF MEETING 2
Observer's Work Sheet

SECTION A

Directions: Each time your partner speaks, make a tally mark in the chart below to show which kind of participation the comment is. (For definitions see "Participant Skills" in Part 1 under the "Participating in Regular Meetings" section.)

Task Skills
(used by my partner)
>Initiating
>Providing information/opinion
>Asking for information
>Clarifying
>Elaborating
>Summarizing
>Compromising

Maintenance Skills
(used by my partner)
>Gatekeeping
>Harmonizing
>Testing norm states
>Encouraging

Other Observations

1. Was my partner's nonverbal participation constructive?
2. Did my partner appear to pay attention to the others as they spoke?
3. Was my partner helpful to the leader?
4. Did my partner act responsibly for the smooth operation of the meeting?

Additional Observations:

SECTION B

Directions: Before the meeting, review the procedures in Part 2 that will be used:

FYI Posters
Agenda Building
Expected Response
Assignment Matrix
+/– Meeting Evaluation

As the meeting proceeds, pay attention to how the procedures are used. When the meeting is over, you will trade places with your partner. With the other observers, you will evaluate the staff meeting by using the +/– Meeting Evaluation procedure.

10: TASK-FORCE REVIEW

Objective

To analyze some problems and come up with recommended solutions.

Process Objectives

1. To practice the basic task-force procedures for problem solving:
   - Build a common information base;
   - Interpret the information base;
   - Achieve resolution.
2. To prepare resolutions for review in a future regular meeting.

Directions

1. The trainer appoints members and a leader for each task force. Each group sits in a circle.
2. The trainer assigns one of the following topics to each task force:
   A. Which of these four Presidents was most effective during his term of office? Johnson, Nixon, Ford, or Carter.
   B. Which of these entertainers has made the most significant contribution to the popular arts? Johnny Carson, Lucille Ball, Bill Cosby, or Mary Tyler Moore.
   C. Which of these individuals, if young and alive, would best qualify for a U.S.-sponsored space colony? Thomas Jefferson, Benjamin Franklin, George Washington, or Paul Revere.

D. What keeps women from becoming President of the United States?

E. What keeps public transportation from being more popular in U.S. urban areas?

F. If medical science could extend the healthy life of a person indefinitely, should we permit it?

G. Max's Meeting (see case study following these directions).

Note: Topics A, B, and C lend themselves to the use of *matrix decision making.* Topics D, E, and F are suitable for application of *force field analysis.* If familiarity with these procedures is not sufficient, participants should stay with the basic procedure outlined in the process objectives. Topic G permits reinforcement of the structure rules in Part 1.

3. The task forces have a twenty-minute time limit. Obviously this will make the quality of the work less than perfect. This effect on quality will in turn challenge the staff meeting that follows. (Twenty minutes.)

4. At the end of the time period, the task-force leader or spokesperson presents the recommendation at a staff meeting for review (Activity 11).

TASK-FORCE REVIEW
Max's Meeting

Alice, Bill, and Carlos report directly to Max and that is why Max always has them in his weekly staff meeting. Dan and Ed both have rapidly growing divisions, and the problems of their growth are almost always on the agenda for Max's meeting, because these problems affect all the rest of the organization. Max believes it speeds up communication if he includes Dan and Ed in the meeting. In Carlos' group, Joe is handling some issues that are politically high profile, and Max invites him to the meeting so that his staff can stay close to these issues until they quiet down. Dan, Ed, and Joe have been attending all of Max's weekly staff meetings for more than six months.

The following figure illustrates the configuration of the meetings.

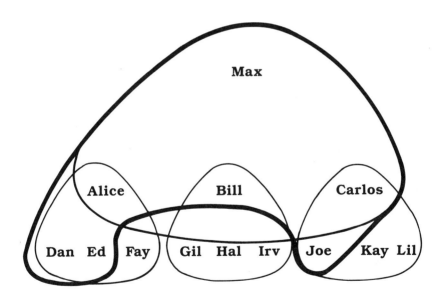

Directions: Discuss the following questions with the other members of your task force. Be prepared to report your answers to the other task forces.

1. What problems might Max be causing with the way he structures the attendance at his regular staff meeting?
2. How might each of the individuals in the chart feel?
3. What recommendations would you give to Max to help him correct the problems you identified?

⇨ *11: RECOMMENDATIONS REVIEW*

Objective

To review the recommendation of a task force. (Use one of the recommended solutions resulting from the "Task Force" activity).

Process Objectives

1. To practice the following procedures for regular meetings:
   - Recommendations Review
   - + / – Meeting Evaluation
2. To be observed and coached by a partner in practicing both task and maintenance skills.

Directions

1. The trainers appoints the members and leader for this staff meeting. This group sits in a semicircle, facing a presentation area.
2. The trainer appoints an observer for each participant in the semicircle. Observers sit outside the meeting semicircle but position themselves to see the face of their partners. (If the group is composed of an odd number, two observers are assigned to one of the participants.) Observers prepare for the meeting by reading the Observer's Work Sheet. (Five minutes.)
3. The leader and participants review the Recommendations Review procedure in Part 2. (Five minutes.)

4. The leader conducts the staff meeting according to the following agenda. (Twenty minutes.)

AGENDA

Items	Procedure	Responsible
Recommendations Review	Recommendations Review	All Participants

5. While the meeting is being conducted, the observers chart their partners' performance in the meeting by using the Observer's Work Sheet. *Members of the meeting should not in any deliberate way create distractions or difficulties for the group or the leader.*

6. After the meeting, each participant meets briefly with his or her observing partner to discuss the notes made in both sections of the Observer's Work Sheet. (Five minutes.)

7. The observers change seats with the participants, taking the inner ring, and evaluate the staff meeting by using the + / – Meeting Evaluation procedure.

RECOMMENDATIONS REVIEW
Observer's Work Sheet

SECTION A

Directions: Each time your partner speaks, make a tally mark in the chart below to show which kind of participation the comment is. (For definitions see "Participant Skills" in Part 1 under the "Participating in Regular Meetings" section.)

Task Skills
(used by my partner)
> Initiating
> Providing information/opinion
> Asking for information
> Clarifying
> Elaborating
> Summarizing
> Compromising

Maintenance Skills
(used by my partner)
> Gatekeeping
> Harmonizing
> Testing norm states
> Encouraging

Other Observations

1. Was my partner's nonverbal participation constructive?
2. Did my partner appear to pay attention to the others as they spoke?
3. Was my partner helpful to the leader?
4. Did my partner act responsibly for the smooth operation of the meeting?

Additional Observations:

SECTION B

Directions: Before the meeting, review the procedures in Part 2 that will be used:

Recommendations Review
+ / – Meeting Evaluation

As the meeting proceeds, pay attention to how the procedures are used. When the meeting is over, you will trade places with your partner. With the other observers, you will evaluate the staff meeting by using the + / – Meeting Evaluation procedure.

Appendix

Following the article on ceremony and power are the answers required for Activities 1, 2, 4, 5, 6, 7.

Ceremony and Power

When I ask managers, "How do you feel about your boss's regular staff meeting?" I usually get a groan in response. It is common opinion, at least among the subordinate participants, that most regular meetings are a boring waste of time.

But a funny thing happens when a manager stops calling such meetings: in about six months, the subordinates start asking for the meetings to be reinstated. They remember how terrible the meetings were, and they admit that they do not have any specific needs for information. Still, they miss their regular meetings.

It is a basic principle of behaviorism that people do not usually go toward something that offers no payoff, and certainly they do not go toward a known source of pain. So, what is going on here? There must be real but hidden payoffs!

If you try to explore this phenomenon by looking into the research about small-group dynamics and process, you will discover a great silence. Very little research has been done about groups and meetings in the context of ordinary organizational operations. Small-group phenomena was mostly studied in the controlled environment of the laboratory. This lab work typically focused on leaderless groups, processing information for purposes of problem solving. Although such settings have immediate relevance for the dynamics and processes of task forces, they are well removed from the weekly staff meeting. The research has little to offer by way of understanding the psychology or sociology of the organization's regular meetings.

I started talking about this curiosity with some of my colleagues in 1983. I especially remember the discussions with Frank Basler and Neal Jensen. We have all been human resources professionals for years, but we also share a further commonality in that we were trained and ordained in our early years as clergymen. Our training for leading worship services probably made it possible for them to take me seriously when I suggested that regular meetings probably had their real motives buried in the psychology of ceremony.

We remembered that throughout most of human history, the mysteries of life were dealt with in spiritual ways. Just as the other mysteries of life in the natural world were identified as spiritual beings, so too were organizations. The primitives recognized the tribe as a powerful reality, distinct from and mysteriously more than could be explained by the spirits of the tribal members. It was symbolized in their totems: "The tribe is real and as different from us as is a bear!" This tribal spirit was acknowledged and its power affirmed and used through tribal ceremony.

Encouraged by my colleagues, I pursued this ceremonial line of reasoning: If the regular meetings in organizations are our secular society's ceremonies, we should find them dealing with the same subjects that ceremonies have always addressed.

Cultural anthropology suggests that there are some common themes or occasions for ceremony in all cultures. They are sometimes called the "rites of passage."[1] These are moments in the life of individual human beings where the community typically intervenes to exercise its presence and authority. They are moments when what is happening to the individual is more than a private thing; it causes change in the lives of many people; it necessitates a community adjustment. In fact, we know that the change in the life of the individual cannot happen at all, or certainly cannot happen constructively, unless the community acknowledges and approves. These are the moments in the life of the individual human being when larger realities—larger spirits—are at work. They are the "sacred" moments. There are some interesting parallels between these realities and those in the life of our organizations.

Almost all cultures recognize at least these seven events as "sacred moments":

Birth	Maturation	Marriage
Leadership	Thanksgiving	Discipline
Sickness and Death		

With the exception of Thanksgiving, all of these moments have in common the fact that they are moments of significant change. Through ceremonies, the community in which the individual lived always intervened to express both its concern and its authority.

---

[1]See *Rites of Passage* by Arnold Van Gennep, 1961, Chicago: University of Chicago Press.

Whether an infant would be raised to maturity, whether a child would be allowed (or required) to take adult responsibility, whether old families could form alliances or new families be formed through marriage, whether one member of the community would be allowed (or required) to exercise unique authority over others, whether uncustomary behavior would be tolerated, whether an ill person would be cared for or the family of the deceased allowed to resume life among the living—all these have always been community decisions. Historically, these decisions have been made final and real through ceremonial action.

Thanksgiving is a little different than other sacred moments. It is the time set aside for the community to acknowledge the forces upon which it knows itself to be dependent—the migration of certain animal species, the sun, fertility, the river, rain, the "one true god," love, or the law. Of all the sacred moments, this is the one most central and most commonly acknowledged in all cultures. Thanksgiving ceremonies are usually the culture's most magnificent ones—the annual or seasonal festivals that last for days or weeks. But they are also the most common and frequent ceremonies—sometimes being performed several times a day.

The word *thanksgiving* has a positive and cheerful connotation for most people. Indeed, joy and revelry have been a part of many thanksgiving ceremonies. But there is a grim side of thanksgiving, too. It is, after all, an acknowledgment of dependency, a subordination of individuals and the whole human community to greater powers. The identification of these powers is a central revelation of the values of the culture. The acknowledgment of their superiority over human life has often been symbolized through sacrifice.

Are the regular meetings within our organizations still doing something like this? Are they still dealing with these kinds of issues? Is it this sort of affirmation of cultural values, organizational reality, and individual roles that are still working through our minds and drawing us into these regular meetings?

After two years of wondering and watching in an informal way, my confidence in the thesis was great enough to persuade the support of Bud Emerson, Director of the San Diego Regional Training Center. A large number of local government agencies are part of this consortium for promoting management development. Bud and others recognized that meetings, especially regular meetings, were one of the most obvious needs for improvement. We were having some success in promoting skill development for leadership of task forces, and we decided to build on that program with a similar set of recommendations about how to lead regular meetings.

We enlisted a band of volunteers and spent our first year recording in detail the issues discussed in more than fifty meetings. We sorted out all the issues where the group did, or attempted to do, problem analysis, decision making, or planning. (I mention "attempts" because it was very clear that regular meetings frequently failed when trying to do this kind of work.) Even with our most conservative (comprehensive) definitions of these cognitive processes, we could barely account for half of the time spent in regular meetings. By our current more precise definitions of the cognitive processes, less than 20 percent of the time spent in regular meetings can be attributed to anything like group problem solving.

Furthermore, we did not have much difficulty sorting the remaining issues into the classic ceremonial agenda:

Birth	Acknowledgment of a new person or idea whose orientation and development needed to be given permission.
Maturation	Recognition that a person or project had achieved a new stage of usefulness that merited new rights and resources.
Marriage	Authorization of a new configuration (restructuring) of the organization's resources.
Leadership	Announcement of promotions, appointments, and assignments.
Thanksgiving	Recognition of acceptable and exemplary performance, and acquisition of key contracts, resources, and support.
Discipline	The identification of unacceptable performance and the determination of penalties.
Sickness and Death	The identification of problems and the allocation of resources for corrective action; the declaration of performance and performer terminations.

In fact, the notes and meetings of our observers during this first year were full of "ah ha's." Not only were the issues recognizable; once recognized most of the rest of the behavior going on in the meetings made better sense. We could better understand why all the managers showed up for the City Manager's Meeting on the morning after each City Council Meeting, and why so much time was spent exploring and joking about "who got shot down this time." After all, most everybody in the meeting was also there the night before, so why spend so much time going over it all again? It is a ceremony for sickness—a healing ceremony—a coming together of the team to lick one another's wounds, put the events into perspective, pick up each other's "spirits" by showing continued respect. "Yes, it was painful, but see: it isn't fatal."

These discoveries at first provided a lot of humor. We could not help seeing the scenes in their more primitive modes, e.g., medicine dances, shotgun weddings, illegitimate ideas taken into the woods and exposed. But by the end of the first year, we were beyond joking. The reality of our thesis was bearing down on us. Every once in awhile we were witnessing moments when the ceremonies were being done well, and we could see that ceremony was powerful medicine.

We saw some awards given with such attention to detail in the review of how it was earned that everyone was instructed and thrilled. We saw months of disruptive action by a renegade manager turned around in a breathtaking moment when the boss said, "You are not dismissed. Take your seat." We saw minds open and wonderful new ideas captured for the organization in which the manager set up a "christening" procedure—a way for new ideas to be presented and taken seriously enough to be given "champions" (parents).

Colleagues in private enterprise were also reporting ceremonial successes. Neal Jensen was especially effective in helping his organization establish deliberate "burial" rites. In his high-tech business, product lines must often be dropped due to obsolescence, and in Neal's organization deliberate times were set aside to monitor the "grief work." Now when the final announcement ("It's over") is made, nobody feels guilty and nobody's career goes into a tailspin. Human energies are refocused, are brought afresh to the accomplishment of new tasks. Turnover is reduced, especially among the precious professional and scientific ranks.

This is strikingly different from many of the other organizations I have been in where years later, engineers are still nursing anxieties because of their involvement with a product that never made it out of R&D or that was short-lived in the marketplace. It is a common recognition among the primitives that a thing improperly buried remains to haunt the community. I think I have seen "haunted" organizations.

In another organization there was an awful silence, and then great relief as one executive suddenly recognized how sacrificial one of there ceremonies was: "Every time we have a couple of bad quarters around here, we restructure. It's terribly disruptive and never really solves anything. Now I see it is ceremonial in nature—a very clumsy healing ceremony where the 'cure' nearly kills. We need some way to get everyone to take the problem seriously that isn't so punishing. We need a better ceremony!"

But perhaps the greatest discovery was how clearly the health of an organization was correlated with the vitality of its regular meetings. Where the ceremonies are right, the organization is doing well! This correlation is no doubt behind the ancient belief that ceremonies are the means by which the gods are allied with the community.

The correlation is probably better explained in secular terms. Regular meetings perform their function well when they:

- Affirm the organization's values—its mission and goals;
- Recreate clarity about the distribution, limits, and relationships of authority;
- Promote role clarity and invite responsible action on the part of the organization's human assets;
- Make certain the organization's successes and failures are identified and the appropriate people rewarded and corrected.

When all this is happening on a *regular* basis, the organization stays organized!

Such meetings are still the best way of keeping the energies of thousands of individuals aligned and focused. They are still the means by which the individual is allowed to transcend himself and to participate in the superior power and intelligence of organizational life.

SCREENING THE AGENDA
FOR REGULAR MEETINGS

The following answers are needed for Activity 1: Screening the Agenda for Regular Meetings and Activity 6: Operations Review Meeting 1.

ANSWERS

Items	Pass Down	Operations Report	Recommen- dation	News	Yes	No
Sample				X	Y-D	
1. Sales		X			Y	
2. Quarterlies	X				Y	
3. Color			X		Y	
4. Shelf			X		Y	
5. Max		X				N
6. Pay	X				Y	
7. Training			X		Y	
8. Turnover		X			Y-D	
9. Alice				X	Y	
10. Z Sales		X			Y-D	

Column group headers: **Items** | **Agenda Type** | **Included?**

Regarding Time

The conservative estimate for all items totals eleven hours and twenty minutes. By delegating the sample item and Items 8 and 10 you have time to resolve all the others. Remember that for the delegated items, time is not the only concern. The quality of problem solving may depend on using employees other than managers on the task force and working in a smaller group.

STRUCTURING MEMBERSHIP OF REGULAR MEETINGS

The following answers are needed for Activity 2: Structuring Membership of Regular Meetings and Activity 7: Operations Review Meeting 2.

ANSWERS

Members	Rationale
Anderson	Department head reporting directly to the City Manager.
Blackwell	Same.
Carlton	Same.
Doolittle	Same.
Englehard	Same.
Finnagan	Same.
Poletti	Same.

Excluded	Rationale
Garcia	Second-level manager; including her would mean including all at second level.
Huskisson	Same.
Ishmaelo	Ambiguous role; largely staff; difficult to justify when excluding important second-level managers.
Jackson	Does not report to the City Manager.
Klopper	Same.
Lovejoy	Second-level manager; including him would mean including all at second level.
Morgan	Same.
Navarro	Same.
Ostrander	Same.
Querles	Same.

Notes:

1. Any of the excluded members might be asked to attend the regular meeting as a special participant, but such invitations should be related to specific issues on the agenda and they should attend only that part of the meeting.

2. Everyone on the list could be included as regular members, but this makes the meeting rather large and will require a lot of formality in the procedures.

   Not all the second-level managers have been included on the list. Additional second-level managers include the Foreman for Parks Maintenance, the Captain of Investigations, the Captain of Fire Prevention, the Head of Word Processing, etc. It is obvious that in this case, the second level of management varies in size of responsibility and in relevance to the general operations of the city.

3. Ishmaelo might be included for a variety of reasons. If he is formally in charge when the City Manager is absent, for instance, it would be good for him to keep abreast of what is happening through regular attendance. At times he exercises authority equal or superior to the Department Heads; but this authority might be best clarified on a case-by-case basis rather than by implying that it is part of his formal role.

IDENTIFYING PARTICIPANT SKILLS

Participant Skills:

A = Initiating   G = Compromising
B = Providing Info. and Opinion   H = Gatekeeping
C = Asking for Info. and Opinion   I = Harmonizing
D = Clarifying   J = Testing the Norm State
E = Elaborating   K = Encouraging
F = Summarizing

The following answers are needed for Activity 4: Identifying Participant Skills.

ANSWERS

__I__ 1. "I'm taking a lot of these questions more personally than I ought to. I'd appreciate a short break while I try to cool off a little."

__A__ 2. "I'd like to shift the group's attention to the potentially negative consequences of the alternatives we are considering."

__B__ 3. "If we go for the first alternative, the follow-on costs will be greater and will probably grow by 10 to 15 percent each year."

__K__ 4. "It's frustrating not having an option that will be popular—which is all the more reason to make sure our conclusion reflects the kind of thorough analysis we've been doing so far and to keep on doing it."

__D__ 5. "When Bob says the follow-on costs of the first alternative will be greater, he means there will be a greater need for software modifications."

__C__ 6. "How do the follow-on costs of these alternatives compare?"

__F__ 7. "So far, we've only been evaluating the negative consequences of the first alternative, and only the follow-on costs have been mentioned."

__G__ 8. "I think we can both the faster hardware of the first alternative and the more stable software of the second alternative. I've heard they are operating compatibly at our plant in Phoenix."

<u>H</u>   9. "How should we interpret your silence on this, Sarah?"

<u>E</u> 10. "If we keep in mind the newness of this vendor, the follow-on costs Bob has mentioned may be even higher."

<u>J</u> 11. "Wouldn't we work more efficiently if we broke into subgroups rather than try to do all of this as one large group?"

PARTICIPANT SKILLS ASSESSMENT

The following answers are needed for Activity 5: Participant Skills Assessment.

ANSWERS

1. The three most frequently abused participant skills that lead to domination of the group:

Asking for information and opinions:

Question asking is the most aggressive of all verbal behaviors. Questions direct others to address what the questioner has in mind. A series of questions turns the exchange into an inquisition dominated by the inquisitor.

Giving information and opinions:

This participant behavior, when overused, simply takes up everyone else's air time. The person overusing this behavior simply talks too much. (If participants had this same problem in mind but selected "Elaborating" rather than "Giving Information," their choice is acceptable.

Summarizing:

This behavior is most often overused by the amateur recorder—an inexperienced person with the flip chart. He or she interrupts after nearly every comment to get it for the record—often changing the verbiage into that of the recorder rather than the participant. Under these conditions, either the summarizer or the group gets strangled.

2. The two participant behaviors that most easily allow a person to empower the participation of other group members are:

Gatekeeping:

Especially when this skill is practiced with grace and respect, it allows any member of the group to invite greater participation from silent but necessary members. It also allows a member to slow down a dominant participant and make air time for others.

Encouragement:

In addition to encouraging a whole group that may be frustrated and discouraged, this behavior can be used to strengthen individual members. To give cautious or shy members sympathetic attention while they speak—eye contact, head nodding, smiling—usually reinforces their willingness to participate.

Note: These answers are generalized from the author's informal observation of many meetings. Certainly within any particular group, other patterns of dominant behavior may be more frequent than these. The author has also seen individuals use the clarifying, elaborating, and summarizing behaviors to empower other members of the group.

START UP STAFF MEETING 1

The following items are the mistakes in the "Pass Down Case Study," which participants were asked to determine in Activity 8: Start Up Staff Meeting 1.

1. There is no way for the members to add items to the agenda.
2. There is no agenda-screening process.
3. The agenda is not prepublished—not sent out ahead of time—so members are possibly unclear about even when or where the meeting is being held.
4. The members are not given time before the meeting to study the related documentation.
5. The agenda is not specific enough to let the members know even what aspects of the topics listed are to be discussed.
6. Expected responses are not indicated on the agenda.
7. The example list shows confusion between the kinds of work regular meetings should do and the kinds of work task forces should do (e.g., "How to stop service complaints").
8. Some of the items on the example list would be better handled in a one-on-one session between the manager and one other member (e.g., the item about report XYZ).

BIBLIOGRAPHY

Bales, R.F. (1950). A set of categories for the analysis of small group interactions. *American Sociological Review, 15,* 257-263.

Benne, K., & Sheats, P. (1948). Functional roles of group members. *Journal of Social Issues, 2,* 42-47.

Beyer, J.M., & Trice, H.M. (1987). How an organization's rites reveal its culture. *Organizational Dynamics,* pp. 5-24.

Daniels, W.R. (1986). *Group power: A manager's guide to using meetings.* San Diego, CA: University Associates.

Deutsch, M. (1960). The effects of cooperation and competition upon group process. In D. Cartwright & A.F. Zander (Eds.), *Group dynamics: Research and theory* (2nd ed.). Evanston, IL: Row Peterson.

Doyle, M., & Straus, D. (1984). *How to make meetings work: The new interaction method* (4th ed.). New York: Berkley.

Grove, A.S. (1985). *High output management.* New York: Random House.

Jones, S.E., Barnlund, D.C., & Haiman, F.S. (1980). *The dynamics of discussion: Communication in small groups* (2nd ed.). New York: Harper & Row.

Likert, R. (1961). *New patterns of management.* New York: McGraw-Hill.

Likert, R. (1967). *The human organization: Its management and value.* New York: McGraw-Hill.

Schein, E.H. (1969). *Process consultation: Its role in organization development.* Reading, MA: Addison-Wesley.

Schein, E.H. (1986). *Organizational culture and leadership: A dynamic view.* San Francisco: Jossey-Bass.

Van Gennep, A. (1961). *Rites of passage.* Chicago: Chicago University Press.